UP THE LADDER

UP
THE
LADDER

Buddhism, Bikram, Bhakti

Donna Lee

Sanctuary Publishing
2016

Sanctuary Publishing
Patagonia, Arizona
© 2016 Donna Lee

Cover Photo by Charmelle Poole, 1982
Cover design by Karen Phillips
Interior design by Vanessa Perez
Priscilla Barton, Editor
Krsna-Kumari Devi-Dasi, Director

ISBN-13:978-0692716274

For more information contact:
donna lee
www.dana-keli.me
donna@dana-keli.me

TO
MY
GURUDEV

CONTENTS

FOREWORD

I have been living within and managing the Hare Krishna temple in Tucson, Arizona for nearly three decades. When Donna Lee first walked through our temple doors, I saw a bright woman who had the confidence to be herself. I immediately realized that she had a profound sense of what she was searching for. Here was an individual whose pursuit of various spiritual paths and personal relationships had blossomed into a deep desire to find ultimate truth–at any price. This requisite determination is described in India's enduring spiritual classic, *Bhagavad-gita,* "Those who are on this path are resolute in purpose, and their aim is one." *[Chapter 2, text 41]*

All of our stories are unique but what sets Donna's story apart is her ability to dive into the recesses of her spirited life with honesty, detachment and deep soul-searching. Donna's account is not a road map for everyone, but offers a candid look into a journey which many will find hauntingly similar to their own efforts and setbacks in the search for spiritual fulfillment.

"*Up the Ladder*" is exactly that–a climb, an upward progression–told with humor, wit, and finesse. This first-hand narration also includes a bit of the remarkable American history of the 1960's intertwined with amusing anecdotes, charming confessions and heroic resilience. Although she didn't intend to write a feminist narrative, Donna's story reveals the naked truth of life in the material world complete with the unfulfilled ambitions, tragedies and the all too familiar compromises women face.

As her life unfolds before us, Donna ends up getting out of the trappings of mundane life through a labyrinth of self-preserving spiritual survival skills. Drawing strength from descended masters and the sacred Vedic writings of India, she overcomes life's upheavals and discovers the truth she has always been seeking. With profound realization, she steadily moves toward a life of pure devotion to God. How significant is this? Again, citing *Bhagavad-gita,* we find the speciality of such people, "After many births and deaths, a person actually in knowledge surrenders unto Me, knowing Me to be the cause of all causes and all that is. Such a great soul is very rare." *[Chapter 7, text 19]*

A.C Bhaktivedanta Swami Prabhupada, the Founder-Acarya of the International Society for Krishna Consciousness, has encouraged all those practicing Bhakti-yoga to record their realizations as a daily exercise. Writing purifies our existence and by sharing our thoughts, we help others along the path. Donna has taken that instruction to heart in "*Up the Ladder*" and is inviting the reader to accompany her in this tale of spiritual discovery. You may encounter a bit of Donna's enigmas in your own life and by emulating her courage and freedom, you, too, can share in her victory of finding peace and satisfaction at last.

Sandamini Devi
Tucson, Arizona
June 21, 2016

INTRODUCTION

According to the founder of the Hare Krishna movement, A.C. Bhaktivedanta Swami Prabhupada, in his purport on text #3, Chapter 6 of the Bhagavad-gita As It Is: "The process of linking oneself with the Supreme is called yoga, which may be compared to a ladder for attaining the topmost spiritual realization. This ladder begins from the lowest material condition of the living entity and rises up to perfect self-realization in pure spiritual life. According to various elevations, different parts of the ladder are known by different names. But all in all, the complete ladder is called yoga and may be divided into three parts, namely jnana-yoga, dhyana-yoga and bhakti-yoga."

Before long, I will be initiated into the Vaishnava culture of Krishna Consciousness. The initiation will put me in direct succession with Krishna's bona-fide gurus. My good fortune makes every cell in my body rejoice. Yet, until I met Giriraj Swami, I was more often than not jaded and miserable.

Always wanting to know the SOURCE of everything, I could not be satisfied. Pleasure did not appease me for long nor did material possessions. Early in my life I recognized the transitory nature of relationships. I knew it was neither fame nor fortune I required. So, what was it that I sought?

We are not a blank slate when we come into this world. We have inclinations and a disposition. And, we have a personality.

My disposition sought yoga as a means to self-realization. Realizing one's eternal nature, sanatana-dharma, requires stripping away the ego that is bound by desire. I have learned that true happiness has nothing to do with having more, getting more or being more. Spiritualists and psychologists agree that Supreme knowledge is the reward for self-realization. True happiness is the gift waiting for us at the topmost rung of the yoga ladder.

My passion for yoga in its various forms was preordained because yoga, as A.C. Bhaktivendanta Swami Prabhupada said, is a means to link with the Supreme and I, determined to know who I am, why I am here, and what purpose I serve, could never give up or give in—nor would I settle for mere appeasements. Through yoga we penetrate Maya, the illusory veil that keeps us attached to the material world. Hatha-yoga is a rung on the yoga ladder. While it is only a step toward realizing the nature of the self, it does show us that mind can overcome matter, while the benefit of practicing asana creates a vibrant vehicle to further the process of self-realization.

As nothing on this planet is free, we cannot simply demand spiritual advancement or imagine our way to self-realization. The circumstances of our life and how we work with them is the path. Each challenge and every bit of unwitting ignorance is an opportunity for advancement. A hard circumstance that we meet with knee-bending humility opens the door to the deepest strata of our being. Self-examination is not only the beginning of yoga; it is also the beginning of wisdom. Each rung of the yoga ladder is a vital step toward something beyond what the ordinary mind might understand. Each step has its rewards, but our perceptions limit us.

How can we know something beyond our experience? Yoga is a way to such knowledge. Along the way, *Up the Ladder* and on the path, I have been high on enthusiasm and my disappointments have shattered me. I have had plenty of association with false gurus and marginal gurus. I spent many years believing that impersonalist philosophies were advanced forms of spirituality. But by the grace of God, I came to Bhakti-yoga and have not looked back.

After numerous years of Buddhist practice and training, I found myself bereft and unsatisfied. Finding the fatal flaw in anyone's teaching or behavior, I would say neti-neti, not this, not that, and then, disappointed once again, remove myself from the situation or guru who was "not it."

Under the guidance of Ajahn Tong, the head meditation master in northern Thailand's Watt Shri Chom Tong, I learned the practice of Vipassana meditation. From Bikram, I acquired a Hatha-yoga practice. From Khenpo Tswang Gyatso Rinpoche and Dzigar Kongtrul Rinpoche, I received Tibetan empowerments. I have traveled once to India with Bikram and once again with His Eminence Dzigar Kongtrul Rinpoche. I have walked on Bimbasara Road, the pathway of the NOBLE ones. I have stood on Vulture Peak. I have sat under the Bodhi tree in Bodhgaya, and in a secret sacred place I received a mind-to-mind transmission from Ani Pema Chodron. As great as all these travels and personages have been, they were still not it. Neti-neti.

With faith in something yet unnamed, I often sat alone, puzzled and confused. The essence of my story is the distillation of these purifying experiences. Neti-neti is an analytical approach to understanding what is eternally abiding by understanding what is not. Therefore, I bow before all those who have served as my guides, teachers and mentors and also those who were 'not it', because each and every step was an opportunity to learn. I honor all pathways and practices, everything and everyone who in their unique way has nurtured my soul. I have never been happier; nor could I believe there is any happiness greater than knowing my place in the divine scheme of things.

While writing this book, I found myself once again in India, at Sacred Govardhan Hill, also known as Giriraj, the King of the Mountains, a place of miracles. I was there by the grace of His Holiness Giriraj Swami, an honored disciple of His Divine Grace A.C. Bhaktivedanta Swami Prabhupada. With faith and service to each, I offer you the story of how I came to navigate the path from Buddhism to Bikram to Bhakti. And, in doing so, I am also happy to serve you, and joyfully be a servant, of the servant, of the Supreme Personality of Godhead.

TIME I AM

"But those who worship Me with devotion, meditating on
My transcendental form—
to them I carry what they lack and preserve what they have."

—*Bhagavad-gita As It Is, 9.22: spoken*
by Yogeshwara Shri Krishna

"Because the moon is full of potentialities, he represents the
influence of the Supreme Personality of Godhead."
—*A.C. Bhaktivendanta Swami Prabhupada*

B ased on the moon's placement in the heavens at the
time of birth, Vedic astrology is one of the meandering
tributaries within the vast tome of knowledge known as the
Vedas. The Sanskrit word Veda, "knowledge or wisdom," is
derived from the root vid-, "to know." To know oneself, why
we are here on this planet, and what our purpose is, are critical
inquiries supported by studying natal astrology.

I appeared in this world when the moon was passing over the eleventh region of the zodiac, Aquarius. This passage has given me artistic gifts and other Aquarian traits such as keen powers of observation, which include seeing beyond the masquerade of false wealth and social position. Aquarius is also the realm of self-sacrifice and renunciation; many ascetics are born under this sign.

Pisces, my rising sign, is in the twelfth house, or last region of the zodiac. In my astrological chart it is Pisces ascendency that has compelled me toward spiritual culmination. For a journey such as mine, coming to Bhakti-yoga is the only conclusion I would find acceptable. From my very first breath, the need to know has shaped my destiny.

My good fortunate comes with Jupiter in the tenth house of Sagittarius because Jupiter's exaltation (in his natural home) has furthered my incessant need to understand and actualize. This location is one of the Mahapurusha yogas, or significant placements. As yoga, it is known as Hamsa, the yoga of the swan or the yoga of discernment. The symbolism of a swan has great significance in Vedic literature. From the Shrimad-Bhagavatam: "As Hamsa he taught the yoga of devotion to you, O Narada." Also from the Shrimad Bhagavatam, Hamsa-yoga is described as follows: "The Vedic Shastras vividly describe how to understand the Supreme Lord, the source of all material and spiritual energy. The swan, or hamsa, is one who discriminates between matter and spirit, who accepts the essence of everything, and who explains the means of bondage and the means to liberation."

Many born under Hamsa-yoga become spiritual leaders, preachers, or teachers because when one attains true knowledge, sharing and love go hand in hand. The honorific given to self-realized masters, paramahamsa, is a theological title applied to renunciates and realized beings who distinguish between the real (sa) and the unreal (ham).

I have been told that Jupiter's exaltation is a lifelong divine blessing and the result of past-life piety. Two beautiful souls in Blagoevgrad, Bulgaria—Abhaya-Mudra Dasi and Patita-Pavan das Adhikary, the Mithuna Twiins—lovingly prepared an extensive astrological package for me. On studying its entirety, I am one-hundred-percent convinced that this small offering, *Up the Ladder*, is in accord with the divine scheme of things.

Last but of utmost importance, Jupiter, benevolently expansive, has an association with the Vedic goddess of good fortune, Lakshmi. Lakshmi, with her golden complexion and four hands, is often seen sitting or standing on a fully bloomed lotus. She is the absolutely devotional wife of Vishnu, the supreme Creator from whom all life begins. And thus, when we put the pieces of our astrological puzzle together in a theological way, we have a map to guide us home.

JEWISH HERITAGE

My need for real knowledge has brought me to the Lotus Feet of the Supreme but not without my share of circumstantial difficulties. Henry Bergson writes, "Fortunately, some are born with spiritual immune systems that sooner or later give rejection to the illusory worldview grafted upon them from birth through social conditioning. They begin sensing that something is amiss, and start looking for answers. Inner knowledge and outer experiences show them a side of reality that others are oblivious to, and so begins their journey of awakening. Each step of the journey is made by following the heart instead of the crowd and choosing knowledge over the veils of ignorance."

I clearly remember being tightly swaddled in baby blankets, unable to turn over or move freely. With the door slightly ajar, I remember having seen the nameless shapes of furniture in the small room. I remember feeling my mother's presence as she approached the door. And, I remember the quiet neurosis that permeated our home.

My birthday also coincides with the anniversary of Kristallnacht, or the Night of Broken Glass, when a massive attack on Jews took place ten years before, in 1938 on November 9th and 10th. Jewish shops throughout Germany, Austria and other Nazi-controlled areas had their windows smashed and businesses looted or entirely destroyed. Synagogues were especially targeted. "That night in Germany, thousands upon thousands of Jews were subject to terror and violence by the Nazis. Over 1,000 Jewish synagogues and over 7,500 Jewish businesses were destroyed, and approximately 30,000 Jewish men were arrested and taken to concentration camps. The name, 'Night of Broken Glass,' comes from all of the shattered glass windowpanes that littered the streets of Germany after the destruction. (Holocaustandhumanity.org) This was the official beginning of Adolph Hitler's campaign to exterminate the Jewish people.

When I was a child, Jews were still in turmoil. Most of our extended family who remained in Eastern Europe did not escape Hitler's death camps. However, the few who did—like my grandparents who emigrated early in the twentieth century—did so, only to enter into a new world. Children of immigrants, as my parents were, wanted desperately to fit in. They were ashamed of being labeled greenhorns, so they did what they could to blend into their youthful American culture. However, their parents were attached to the old ways and the old world, making their children unable to join in the pastimes their peers enjoyed. For instance, my father was not allowed to play on sports teams or sing in the choir. These extracurricular activities were considered a waste of time. My grandparents and surviving relatives, damaged by the war and its aftermath, were fearful and ever on guard for the interloper who might begin to chip away at the defining, iron-clad religious and cultural conditioning they desperately wanted to bestow on their children.

My father arrived in America from Poland when he was six years old. His mother, a radical Zionist, and her rabbinical husband were considered politically dangerous by Polish authorities and suspected of anti-establishment activities. My grandmother, a robust, opinionated woman who hid from the officials, was secreted out of the country before the Polish government could sequester her. When my paternal grandparents came to America and resettled in Hartford, Connecticut, they were both still active in Zionist politics.

I remember my grandmother as a short, stout woman with long gray hair that she kept neatly braided in the wrapped fashion that was popular then. She had large breasts that melded into her thick waistline, all hidden by the aprons she wore. She, like my maternal grandmother, added blue tint to her gray hair, which gave them both an eerie appearance.

My grandfather, with his blue eyes and large hearing aid that protruded from his left ear, had a scholarly persona. After saving for some time, Aaron and Clara were able to purchase a three-family home on a busy street in Hartford. When my oldest aunt married, she and her husband and my twin cousins lived in the first-floor apartment, ready for Clara's command.

I frequently visited my grandparents. We lived behind them on a more affluent, tree-lined street with single-family homes. Conveniently, I was able to cut through a neighboring backyard, whereupon I entered into a bustling busy street with bus lines that ran in either direction. We always used the back stairway to enter Aaron and Clara's home. The stairway was significant to me, as it was a dark tunnel into another world.

When I opened the back door, I would see my grandmother's clique sitting around a large wooden kitchen table, with melting sugar cubes between their teeth, drinking their tea in the Russian style. In the next room, also visible from the back entrance, I would see my grandfather seated at the head of another large table with mysterious large books spread out before him. He studied *Talmud* (Jewish literature) and wrote poetry in Yiddish for the local Jewish publications. To avoid being swept into a political maelstrom, he would turn his hearing aid down to not hear his wife shouting her political views while pounding her fist on the kitchen table.

My father was the oldest son of five children. He began to support his rabbinical family with a paper route when he was just eight years old. From then on, he was expected to contribute to the family's welfare. He took his role as breadwinner very seriously. With responsibility placed on him at a very young age and denied the development of his natural gifts (music), he developed lifelong nervous conditions and had extreme bouts of depression.

My mother's parents emigrated to the U.S. from Russia. They also escaped the pogroms, the wave of anti-Jewish sentiment that swept the Ukraine early in the twentieth century. My mother often told me how her mother, my maternal grandmother and her sister tied themselves together with bed sheets, afraid that they would go overboard during the ocean crossing. They came across the Atlantic when they were teenagers, saying good-bye to their parents, friends and other relatives knowing they might never see them again.

My mother's parents, both from the same village in Russia, did not meet until they arrived in New York at Ellis Island. The familiarity of their background was a firm foundation for a loving marriage. After a brief stay in New York, they moved to New Britain, Connecticut where they established themselves in a small Jewish community with a junk business. This turned into a lucrative scrap metal business that morphed into a very lucrative coal and oil business.

My maternal grandmother was far kinder and gentler than my father's mother. She dressed nicely and wore the tasteful jewelry that my grandfather purchased for her. My maternal grandfather always wore three-piece suits with a gold watch on a heavy chain in the pocket of his waistcoat.

My mother had four older brothers and adored each one of them. My mother, Helen, had the sweetest nature and was a natural beauty. When I was grown and trying to make sense of our family history, one of my aunts told me that, as young woman, my mother was noticeably out of touch with what went on around her, always in a world of her own that was filled with table settings and fashion.

My paternal grandmother had ambitions for her son, Benjamin. She wanted him to marry into an established Jewish family. She wanted him to earn the means to see his brother and sisters also established in marriages and businesses. My mother, Helen Rebecca Gittleman, was the chosen bride. Although my mother was in love with someone else, her marriage to my father was arranged.

When I would stare at mother's wedding picture, I saw a slim, winsome bride in a sophisticated white-silk gown. She held a small bouquet of flowers and wore an enigmatic smile that created a Mona Lisa mystery. My mom kept the wedding album stashed away in the dining-room credenza but I would pull it out to study these people who were my parents. Seeing me with the album in my hands, she would repeatedly tell me that she knew marrying my father was a mistake.

Helen believed that family life was meant to look like the cover of one of the ladies' magazines she always kept neatly stacked by her bedside. But I promise you, our family was anything but material for Good Housekeeping or the Ladies' Home Journal.

The marriage was not a good match for either Helen or Ben. My father's hot temper and nervous conditions were unsuitable for my mother's naturally sweet innocence. They were not young when they married. Helen, already thirty-one, would soon be considered an old maid by the standards of that time. My father was six years older.

After prohibition and with his mother's firm insistence, Ben opened a liquor store in the south end of Hartford. Never disobeying his mother or finding her tyranny unacceptable, he did as he was told. He was one of the many who daily sat around Clara's large table, receiving her benedictions and admonishments.

Every day except Sunday he shamefully sold alcohol to the poor black people who lived in Hartford's slums. His work did nothing to uplift his spirits, yet the business of selling spirits did support his siblings and he was able to send his youngest brother to pharmaceutical college and establish other businesses for his brothers-in-law.

While my father ran his business and met with his mother daily, my mother spent her time reading her ladies' magazines, trying to make a home that would be picture perfect. Her head was filled with casseroles, table settings and well-dressed children. When her husband came home from a day and night of liquor sales and his mother's tongue-lashing denunciations, he would be intolerably brusque, dispelling Helen's dreams the moment he walked though the door.

My brother, Alan, was born in 1945. My aunts told me that Alan was the most beautiful baby any of them had ever seen. He was the first grandchild born into my father's large family. He had blond curls, blue eyes and was welcomed into the family like a long-awaited prince. Soon enough, though, Alan became a problem and exhibited signs of a malevolent personality disorder. I was terrified of him.

I entered the world with sanskaras (impressions or imprints) on my mind that gave me a particular and often inexplicable point of view. As a child, I recalled another lifetime. I remembered a place where—free from restraint—I walked on a high cliff above a river's edge. I often dreamed of dancing in a temple, hearing bells ring, and being dressed in colorful exotic clothing.

As a young girl, I imagined pilgrimages either on foot or on horseback. I would spend the day in reverie, sitting astride my imaginary horse, riding in gorgeous canyon landscapes, combating difficulties, questioning authorities and ultimately being the heroine in my story. I loved climbing on the roof of an old garden shed with my dearest boy cousin and riding my bike on grand adventures.

Often alone, I was not lonely. I used my time imaginatively and thought deeply about the people I observed. I had a playroom on the third floor of our old house where I frequently sat by the windows, watching my parents and brother quarreling on the driveway below. We lived in a three-story brick house with a rambling front porch, but the house also had a frightening personality. It was old and creaky and sounded as if it were moaning. My brother would add to my terror by telling me stories of the invisible people who lived in that house. He would tell of murderers and rapists who loved little girls my age. Only three years older than I, he knew horrible things and delighted in them.

Usually ignored by the adults, I was able to listen and observe without consequence. One conversation my mother had with her sisters-in-law concerned my paternal grandmother's brother. He had escaped from a concentration camp, and for nearly three years he hid, with others, underground in foxholes. I heard the women whisper about how they would come to the surface each night to scavenge for potatoes or whatever else they could find to ward off starvation. No one gave a thought to my presence nor could they imagine that such a young child would comprehend their conversation.

The women went on to discuss ways to raise money to bring him to America and help him get established. My aunt Edith was vehement. She said, "I do not want my children to know anything about this," in reference to the suffering the Holocaust survivors had endured.

I was all ears and could not imagine why she would not want her children to know this enthralling story. It became even more powerful when I learned that he married one of the women with whom he escaped and that they had lost, in all, eight children and their respective spouses to Hitler's atrocities. After surviving underground together, they married while exiled in France.

I did not understand the world I found myself living in, and neither did I understand the callousness that I had perceived. When my relatives finally arrived in the United States, I saw two people who had the capacity to love and go on living despite their tragedies.

Even though I was very young, I recognized a tenderness in these people that was unlike any qualities I had thus far experienced. A few years later at a family picnic, Sylvia, my great-uncle's war bride, crowned me with a wreath of wild flowers. It was a tender, loving moment for me—a neglected child who went unnoticed and uncared-for by self-absorbed, damaged, narcissistic parents and a demonic, terrifying brother.

BEAT

I had nothing to offer anybody except my own confusion.
—Jack Kerouac

Later, like so many in my generation impacted by the events of the 1940's and the pursuant bland denial years of the 1950's, I was drawn toward philosophies and Eastern religions in search of understanding and perspective. As a young teenager, I first identified with the beat generation. I dreamed of being on the road with Jack Kerouac. Internally, I experienced the wave of changes that swept America from the 1950s and well into the hippy years. Though very young, I had an uncanny way of knowing who was at the forefront of art and mind-expanding changes. Later on, in Miami, I was fortunate to hear Allan Ginsburg recite his most famous poem, *Howl.*

I was certainly rebellious, loving art and poetry and the newly emerging folk music. I let my hair grow long like the folk-singers I admired. I kept to myself, listening to Joan

Baez's early albums on a brown record player. It sat on the floor of my room with the albums I repetitiously played, stacked neatly by its side. I loved the English ballads as well as Harry Belafonte's island sound and Odetta's African click song. I smoked cigarettes, snuck into coffee houses in downtown Hartford, and thought deeply about spirituality. Without encouragement, I wrote poetry. The opening line of a first poem went something like this: For every saint there is a sinner, run sinner run...

I was very daring. One Saturday, all by myself, I took the train from Hartford to New York City, where I walked the streets, peering into windows and gawking at the endless streams of people. Toward day's end, I came to an art gallery not far from Grand Central Station. A Margaret Keene print hung in the window. The painting, entitled Alone, depicted one of the artist's big eyed-waifs alone on a floating staircase, aloft in a midnight-blue sky.

I desperately wanted that print. It was the first time I saw a representation of my state of being, my person-hood. That very moment was the birth of a lifelong interest in painting, portraiture and printmaking.

Without sufficient money to purchase it, I left New York City by the evening train and returned to my bland suburban, troubled home. I had to confess where I'd been all day and, to my surprise, my mother uncharacteristically agreed to take me back to New York the very next week and buy me the print.

I was fourteen or fifteen years old. The Keene print caused me to rethink my bedroom. Painting the walls and ridding myself of childish furniture, I created a new environment with a daybed that resembled a sofa and one black dresser. I created a minimalist room where the Keene print could take center stage. Like the little waif, I rimmed my eyes with dark kohl and wore clothing my mother abhorred. I groped my way through situations and circumstances without supervision or guidance. Alone.

A CHILD BRIDE

My fate was sealed when I met Michael in the eighth grade. He and I spent many hours debating life and existential philosophies. I had turned into a sexy young teenager who loved to wear black tights, walk barefoot and read whatever esoteric material I could find.

My offbeat, independent beatnik appearance attracted Michael and he and his family fascinated me. His mother was an eccentric woman. His father, an artist, had passed away before I had the chance to meet him. His paintings and the home he designed and built spoke to my not-yet-realized artistic nature.

Michael's mother, Rhoda, allowed him to drive when he was only fourteen. She sent him on errands and allowed him to hitchhike from Connecticut to Washington, D.C. where his older brother lived with his wife and child. These things flabbergasted me. In contrast, my mother thought that every turn in the road was dangerous and adventures happened only in her magazines.

I hated school and its factory-like long narrow hallways. I hated the ringing bells and the slamming lockers jarred my sensitivities. I avoided the gymnasium and the screaming kids who rooted for their basketball team. Noise was intolerable. One day, I walked in the front door of the school and walked right past my locker and continued down the hall, down the stairs, and out the back door. I went home. I walked into the house and told my mother I could no longer attend school. She said nothing. I began to realize that I was freer than I previously thought.

The year Michael turned sixteen his mother bought him a funky old car. He would pick me up in the morning and, with a fabulous lunch packed by my mom, we'd skip school and drive to the Connecticut shore where he and many of his friends had closed-up beach cottages. We usually didn't have enough money for gas and we'd scrape together the last cents we had to make our way home.

At that time, gas was thirty cents a gallon. I spent my tenth grade year driving around New England with Michael, smoking cigarettes, visiting the beautiful Rhode Island beaches, and going into the mountains of New Hampshire and Vermont.

Somehow, he managed to get by in school and he graduated. As for me, at the tender age of sixteen, on the very day that I failed my driver's test, I passed my pregnancy test. Consequently, my parents and my future mother-in-law decided that Michael and I should marry. Since we were accustomed to long drives, they packed us off to Maryland, a state open to legitimizing the marriages of children.

My mother was concerned about what I would wear to my ridiculous secret courthouse wedding. So we went shopping and chose a teal-blue suit with suede insets in the jacket to make me look older and more respectable. Michael was only seventeen and about to attend the University of Miami. There was never any talk about my having an abortion or staying home or going to a sheltered environment or finishing high school.

With the death of Martin Luther King, my father's business in the heart of Hartford's poverty-ridden slums was looted and burned. At the same time, my brother Alan's dangerous schizophrenic personality disorder became a dark force in our home.

My parents were unequipped for their lives, the changing times, and their troubled children. Therefore, my mother and father thought it best to relocate me far away from this madness with no consideration that I was not ready for a life without protection or supervision. I would be out of sight and out of mind.

Never showing me any kindness or speaking directly to me, my father did manage to say: "You're nothing but a brat and you've never been anything other."

With that benediction, Michael and I were swiftly relocated to Miami, Florida, where Michael attended school and I, at sixteen, was left to fend for my pregnant self in a strange big city. Swooning with prenatal diabetic sugar shock, I vividly remember going to the obstetrician in downtown Miami and almost fainting on the corner of Brickell Avenue. Of course, I knew nothing about pregnancy or self-care, let alone about mothering an infant. Going to the OB/GYN alone was just one of the assaults on my developing person-hood.

With our parents' financial support, we rented a small apartment in Coconut Grove, Florida, a place that in 1965 offered a relaxed bohemian atmosphere. During the day, Michael attended his university classes. I spent the day walking through Coconut Grove, looking at art and the boats on the bay. During the night, he roamed the streets, eating at late-night greasy spoon restaurants and coming in long after I had gone to bed.

With a new life growing inside of me, I was unrecognizable to myself. This phenomenon signaled the beginning of an understanding that I was not my changing body. As my belly swelled, so did my face. My features changed drastically. Maternity clothes were ugly. Who was I? I spent considerable time in front of the mirror contemplating my unrecognizable self.

My daughter, Jill, was born on November 2, 1965 at Mount Sinai Hospital in Miami Beach. She weighed in at eight and one half pounds. The birth was difficult. I wasn't prepared. I had a spinal block and awoke from the anesthetics, screaming that I could not feel my legs. After I vomited for hours in the recovery room, they finally put Jill into my arms. I didn't know what to make of this little bundle of life. I had no experience with babies nor did I have any help when I returned home from the hospital. Michael continued attending university classes while I tried to make sense of my life and care for Jill as best I could.

The courage to say the truth was one of my first spiritual practices. So, when asked if I was the babysitter, I would ardently respond—"No! I am her mother." I remember one incident in a grocery store where the cashier would not believe me and made a scene in front of the many shoppers who were in line behind me. I would not back down. Though she was a baby, Jill had ears and needed the same ferocity and protection that I desperately needed.

The African proverb, "It takes a village to raise a child," did not apply to my child or me. I was a child raising a child, with no community, no family, and no one nearby to help me. There was no one to guide and educate me or to teach me how to cook and feed my daughter or myself. I was swimming upstream against all odds. Scraped against the rocks and bruised by the obstacles, I was the pearl hidden within the oyster's shell. Alone. With an impressive resolve and no choice, I kept going.

When my daughter was a toddler, I spent many long days taking her to the tourist attractions in the greater Miami area. We went to the zoo, the Monkey Jungle, the aquarium and any other child-related environment I could find. Having no companionship or guidance, I just didn't know what else to do.

Toward Michael's graduation in 1968 or 1969, his progressive sociology professor, Calvin Leonard, returned from a human-potential seminar on the West Coast. Once back in the classroom, Professor Leonard threw the textbooks out and revamped his class. Teaching his students to be expressive and real was more pressing than learning dead material from old textbooks.

Michael came home raving about this new wave of honest communication, referred to as sensitivity training or encounter groups. I was invited to attend Professor Leonard's first encounter group in Florida. With caring guidance, he encouraged us to face one another and begin revealing ourselves. Skillfully, Calvin Leonard began to teach us honest communication. I was hungry for any association that recognized my person-hood.

Close to finishing his requirements for graduation, Michael packed up and left us, with no intention of returning. He was offered an internship at Esalen Institute. With his focus on the blossoming human-potential movement, I was again left to fend for myself.

Because I had no associations with people my age, other than those brief meetings at the University, I was once again alone in a big city with a small daughter. Jill and I moved to a different part of town. I sent Jill to the morning sessions at a Montessori school so that I could attend Miami-Dade Junior College. I was nineteen years old. My mom's father died when Jill was born, leaving me a small but considerable sum for those days. With fourteen thousand dollars I was able to support Jill and myself for a while. I bought a brand-new beige Volkswagen bug for nineteen hundred dollars.

It's hard to fathom how I could have been on my own but I was too naïve to be very aware or to know anything else. Though my circumstances were very different, for the first time in many years I began to associate with people my age. We lived in an apartment building near the campus in a not-very-nice neighborhood. I did well in school. During that time, I met an attorney who helped me attain a divorce.

Jill and I drifted along for a while until, out of the blue, I received a phone call from Michael insisting we come West to experience the blossoming human-potential movement. He was at Kairos in Southern California, an Esalen-type growth center, and wildly excited about his experiences. I repeatedly turned down his pleading invitations but eventually he won me over.

HIPPY TIMES

I packed the car, closed the apartment, and Jill and I drove west. When we arrived in Rancho Santa Fe at Kairos, Michael said, "Okay, you're here, and now you must find your own lodging and make your own way."

Dumbfounded by this turn of events I stood motionless, letting the words sink in, and quickly realized that he had a new girlfriend. It was something I had never considered. During each phone call that he made from California he begged to see his daughter. When I finally arrived at Kairos, where he lived and worked, I had hoped that he would assume responsibility for Jill thinking his incessant pleadings for us to come west stemmed from so-called fatherly devotion.

That afternoon, with no ulterior motive, a senior employee at Kairos kindly allowed us to spend the night at his place. The next day, he hired me as the receptionist. My job was to welcome workshop participants, see to their rooms, and collect their money while being exceptionally gracious. As I saw to the guests, Jill played on the grounds with the owner's four children.

The atmosphere suggested a moneyed, casual elegance that I was unfamiliar with. Nothing about the environment was reminiscent of the Jewish neurosis I was accustomed to. People appeared to be comfortable in their skin. It was my first awareness of just how much emotional baggage I carried.

Eucalyptus trees and cozy bungalows surrounded Kairos's primary building. Jill and I often slept on the floor in front of the main room's massive stone fireplace while some employees took acid and danced the night away to Santana and Leon Russell.

Introduced to groundbreaking psychological approaches, I met many leaders in the forefront of the then-experimental humanistic psychology movement. I felt fortunate to be in the company of Laura Huxley, Alan Watts, Gary Snyder, Stanley Kellerman, and Abraham Maslow, to name just a few.

First-generation students of Fritz Perl's also introduced me to Gestalt Therapy. I met Richard Brautigan and listened to him read from his humorous book, *A Confederate General from Big Sur.* One of my former Beat heroes, Alan Watts, did rituals while getting drunk on straight vodka. He came for a weekend with Gary Snyder who read groundbreaking ecological poems. I also discovered the work of Big Sur poet, Robinson Jeffers.

I was getting a first-class education after all. It was an exciting, expansive time and I thought it to be a healthy environment for my young daughter. Though we were often homeless, shifting from one locale to another, we were always close to the Self-Realization Fellowship on the cliffs high over the Encinitas shoreline. Like many of my generation, Paramahansa Yogananda's *Autobiography of a Yogi* had a tremendous impact on me. As I turned the pages of the book, I was captivated by everything I read about India.

Along with experiencing the human-potential movement's radical therapeutic modalities, I also attended the Sunday service at Yogananda's Self-Realization Temple while Jill attended the children's program. At that time, Jill and I lived communally in Del Mar in an old funky house. It was at the top of a high hill with an ocean view from the glass room perched precariously on the flat roof.

Jill was an adorable child, with long curly black hair and brown eyes. She looked a lot like her father. I taught myself to sew on a borrowed machine and loved making my daughter hippy-style clothing. Our home was an old bakery truck that we fixed into a camper. It had a huge slanted front window with enough room to make a cozy bed right beneath the window for little Jill. We had a small cook-top stove and we used the bathroom in the house.

Other members of our little family included a jeweler who made custom rings and bracelets as well as a few guys who were roadies for the Quick Silver Messenger Service, a rock band famous in the late 1960s. Our tribe also included a few young men whom Tom Wolfe had written about in *The Electric Kool-Aid Acid Test* and *The Pump House Gang*.

One of our communal members, Skip Taylor, was considered a medicine man. Skip was anything but what he appeared to be. He had a short blond crew cut and drove an older Mercedes sedan with a tennis racket sitting on the shelf under the back window. With that classic car and its collegiate emblem on the bumper, Skip went from Indian reservations to Laguna Beach, from east to west, dispensing hallucinogenic mind-altering substances. Skip often got LSD directly from Timothy Leary's "Brotherhood of Eternal Love" in Laguna Beach. One Saturday night, Skip was liberally dispensing the acid to anyone who wanted to trip. Forewarned that it was powerful medicine, I took a large dose. When the LSD came on, I sat in front of the fireplace for eight hours in a crossed-legged meditation seat, with a hologram-type image of Paramahansa Yogananda appearing continuously in the flames.

The next morning I went to the service at SRF. The monk who spoke started out by saying something along these lines: LSD is medicine for our times but when you have come to your realizations, it's time to get on with your work and begin to live your life purposely. The medicine has worked and you need no more!

Was I stunned? Yes, of course, and I took the message seriously, realizing that if I continued to live as I was, I would not advance on the path. I didn't know what the path was or where I wanted to go. I only knew that he had spoken to me and I had work to do.

I felt compelled to spend time with my parents. They desperately needed my love and I, still a child with a child, desperately needed them. I knew I had to start at the beginning, rewinding. Hippy life was appealing but an inner voice said move on.

My parents' lives went from one tragedy and mismanaged affair to another. Finally, they escaped the torment of my brother's dangerous schizophrenic personality disorder and tumultuous times by selling all their belongings and leaving conservative New England to resettle in the Jewish enclave of Hallandale, Florida.

LIKE AN INDIAN MARRIAGE: NO CHOICE

I wanted to bring my parents any happiness I could. Limited in their thinking, they were Old School, believing that a woman's only worth was in her marriage and her husband's prestige. No husband. No prestige. No worth. It was that simple for them.

My divorcing Michael after they supported us for so many of his college years disappointed my father. He assumed Michael would take over supporting Jill and me as soon as he graduated. There was never any discussion about my becoming independent or having a life other than as someone's wife.

Away from the pressures of his business and my brother's threatening presence, my father's otherwise harsh personality softened somewhat. He wasn't exactly pleased to have me back and yet he wasn't altogether opposed to my re-entry either. They lived in a one-bedroom apartment. I slept on the sofa and Jill slept on a hideaway cot. She cleverly made the second bathroom into her playroom.

I got a job as a receptionist in a law firm and my parents were delighted to look after Jill. I put away my hippy clothing and tried on a new look. I wasn't crazy about this new me but it made my parents happy.

My father played golf with a man who also lived in the apartment complex. This man had a friend whose son had moved to Miami and worked for one of the top seven accounting firms, Cooper & Lybrand.

My father's friend wanted to fix me up with his friend's son. My dad kept putting him off but one day he reconsidered and said to me, "Donna, Al would like you to meet a young man. Would you consider going out with him?" I was surprised that my father was acting friendly toward me, and so, of course, I said yes.

The new me on the scene was slim, attractive, athletic and tan from the Florida sun. I had strong, shapely legs and loved to swim and bike ride and walk on the beach. I still wrote a bit of poetry and had my head in esoteric books. I tried to disguise my natural Bohemian inclinations and they came to light just enough to make my good looks and quirky personality interesting to Bob who was straight as an arrow and had little experience beyond his home court.

Bob played sports in college and joined the ROTC to reduce his chance of being sent to Vietnam. After only a few dates, he asked me to marry him. I was twenty-five and he was twenty-six.

He was tall and thin with blue eyes and light hair. Bob was coached by his dad all through his athletic career and drafted by the New York Mets while still in high school. Unable to negotiate the contract to his father's liking, he turned down the offer and continued on with his education, becoming a star on his college basketball and baseball team.

My parents were thrilled with his clean-cut Jewish background and put together a book of his press clippings and achievements. They were sure I had struck gold, and we were a striking couple. Everyone except his mother was delighted for us.

Our fathers arranged the marriage. I felt as though I had no choice. I wanted to make amends for my teenage pregnancy and the aggravation I caused. Lost and adrift, with no education or skills and a young daughter, I married the man of their choice. I thought I was invulnerable. We married quickly in the attorney's office where I worked.

We were to have another Jewish wedding with my grandfather officiating as soon as Bob's parents could make the trip from Pennsylvania to Florida. Bob and my mother wanted me to have a flashy diamond ring but all I wanted was a sewing machine. I made Jill's dress for the upcoming wedding, which took place in my folks' apartment. I wore a red knit dress.

The whole thing was ridiculous and Bob's mother hated me right away. In some ways I felt as though I deceived him, yet only as much as I innocently deceived myself. I thought I could be anything he wanted. I didn't know then that I had a profoundly artistic nature and a spirit that needed to know where it came from and why. He didn't know that his love of money would eventually ruin his life.

Bob and I were both culturally conditioned. I wanted to please. He wanted to amass wealth and live comfortably without questioning why he was here on this planet or what greater purpose his life served. Money was his motivation.

Within a few months of our marriage I was pregnant with our first son, Adam. I joyously welcomed the pregnancy. With a loan from one of Bob's relatives, we purchased a sweet little house near the beach in Hollywood's South Lake neighborhood.

A year later our second son, Jeremy, was born. I pictured myself as an earth mama with a household of children and home-baked bread and all the trimmings that went with my previously romantic view of hippydom.

From the very beginning Bob and I had different goals and our varied perspectives did nothing to create the family unity that I so dearly desired. When Adam was born Bob became harsh and critical, not unlike my own father, and he often treated his stepdaughter, Jill, with cold-hearted disapproval. Unfortunately, she began to despise him; I had to accept that *happy ever after* would not be the end of our story.

Although I tried, I could not break through Bob's rock-hard images of Jehovah's institutions. *In God we trust*, he continued to invest, even though I knew that money would not bring us happiness. Bob stubbornly refused to pay heed to the numinous illuminations of my omens. He continued to amass wealth while I continuously searched for greater meaning. I knew there was something beyond material success. I was, though not consciously and not with any external support, at the bottommost rung of the yoga ladder. I needed to know what lay behind the veil of delusion. Like most people, however, I was caught in *Maya's* sticky web.

WESTWARD

Florida's claustrophobic boulevards, jammed with endless streams of traffic and strip malls, restaurants and amusements, did not support the way I wanted our children to see the world. I wanted an environment that would encourage all of us to be resourceful and creative.

Our neighbors from Spokane extolled the beauty and virtues of the Northwest. I was drawn to pictures of Mount Ranier and Seattle's climate promised relief from Florida's outgoing, have-more-fun tourist nature. Investigating, I soon discovered an idyllic spot, Bainbridge Island, only a thirty-minute ferry ride across Puget Sound into downtown Seattle.

Excited by the prospect of a different lifestyle, Bob was able to secure a job with A Thousand Trails, in Seattle as the company's financial comptroller. Though my parents were devastated when hearing the news of our move, at that point our young family's future was most important. I knew that in Florida the children's lives would be stamped from a mold.

Knowing that everyone's creativity could flourish on Bainbridge Island, we bought a small house that was perched on a wooded ravine on a dead-end lane. Although the house was small, it had cathedral wood ceilings throughout and floor-to-ceiling architectural windows in the living room. We installed a wood stove in the existing fireplace and in that cozy room looking out over the second-floor deck, I set up a weaving studio.

In the autumn, a huge old maple tree turned the living and dining area a brilliant orange. The house was filled with warmth and texture. My finished work—woven clothing, interesting dolls, wall hangings and more—created a cozy nest. We placed an upright piano for Jeremy at one end of the room.

Rachel, our fourth child, was born at home on Penny Place. We then hired a local architecture student to design a renovation for the small house. It became unique with a curved stairway leading to an attic loft for the boys and a studio for me in the downstairs daylight basement. Jill was in the public middle school, and Adam and Jeremy went to the Montessori school.

The island was enchanting. Homes were nestled far off the road, protected by dense foliage, and the constant light rain encouraged quiet, thoughtful times. Bob supported us by crossing the sound each morning with hordes of others who worked in the city and returned each night. In the winters when the days were short, the work force never saw the island in daylight.

The Bainbridge years were the happiest in our marriage. While my children were young and enjoying the natural settings on the island, my artistic nature had time and space to develop and the boys had plenty of room to roam and run with the other neighborhood kids on the hillside across from our house. When working on my loom, I overheard imaginatively creative play from the youngsters playing happily in the nearby wooded ravine. Bob spent as many hours as he pleased coming and going.

As I wove my cloth, I imagined myself as an independent woman with a successful business. The Goodfellow Catalog of Wonderful Things was seeking profiles of artists and their respective crafts. I needed to create a portfolio so I hired a photographer to take pictures of myself wearing my creations and asked my friend, Diane, if we could do the shoot at her fabulously artistic home. The cover photo on this book is one of those PR shots from my portfolio. I applied with my colorful presentation and was accepted. Thereafter, I was invited to New York to show my work at the Wool Bureau. In turn, they sent me to a textile-design firm which, in turn, sent me to the office of the fabric editor at Vogue magazine.

Riding in a taxi on Madison Avenue to Vogue was a scene in my mind's ongoing movie. I was somebody. I loved being dressed in fabrics and clothing I had made. I loved carrying a large black portfolio case in New York City. I loved being a creative person on a mission. Although I thought it was a business I was after, it wasn't.

Sensibly, I had to choose my family over living in New York and pursuing a career that would have been improbable. I wasn't attracted to material success. I was after the acknowledgment that I was talented and that my work was, after all, art. Coming back to the island, I was enthused about opening a textile studio in Lynwood Center, a quaint section of Bainbridge Island but, soon, I began to realize the futility of that endeavor. Neti-neti

JEW'BU'S

Cloistered by forests and surrounded by Puget Sound, Bainbridge Island was an ideal locale for families that appreciated privacy and variety. One good soul, Janet Hanrahan, invited everyone with Jewish connections to her home for a late-fall Hanukkah party. News of the get-together spread via the grapevine and for many of us it was the beginning of valuable friendships. (That party was the cornerstone of Bainbridge Island's now-formalized Jewish community.)

After the party we began to come together to observe and celebrate the Jewish holidays in an ecumenical way, with what we thought of as a Buddhist mindset. None of us realized the impersonal nature of Buddhism. We knew it as a non-violent, mindful philosophy with exotic and intriguing elements. The Japanese Buddhist monks who were stationed on the island encouraged our views. They spent their days walking along the main roads and mindfully beating drums to protest the development of a Trident submarine base proposed for the nearby Olympic Peninsula.

Coining the expression JewBu's, we encouraged everyone to contribute to our gatherings in whatever way they could. Many of us had young children and, in this way, we frequently came together. The seasons changed and the children grew. Around the time Rabbi Ira Stone came to the island to give a series of talks, Rachel was ready for kindergarten and Adam and Jeremy were entering middle school. Jill was about to graduate from high school. As a family we had gone through many growth cycles and transformations. I had not yet found the answers to my life's questions and Rabbi Stone made an impression on me.

As lovely as Bainbridge was, I was ready to leave and move in closer to the rabbi's congregation to see if a more traditional Jewish life would satisfy me. I craved a structured avenue of spiritual expression and Ira Stone was a serious man who was passionate about revivalist Judaism. His depth intrigued me. I was hungry for real knowledge and knew my talent for clothing design and attempts at business were not it. Neti-neti.

I wanted a spiritual life that was a full expression and what I've now come to realize as reciprocal. I wanted to stop speculating. I wanted to know something seemingly unknowable. And, I wanted my children to learn how to navigate the world. I thought Bainbridge Island's isolated, idyllic lifestyle would not prepare them for their independent lives. If we were to stay there, all I had to look forward to would be a stagnant comfort zone.

After Jill's high school graduation, we arranged for her to live on an Israeli kibbutz. I felt her choices in the Pacific Northwest were limited and going to Israel would give her experiences and opportunities that a community-college education could not provide.

The day Bob took her to the airport was a breech in our relationship that even these many passing years have not healed. The pain of what seemed like an abrupt separation tore me up. When the car pulled away, I put on running shoes and ran around Battle Point Park's running track until I could not take another breath or run another step.

To this day, she doesn't realize the courage it took to send her off. After all, she had been my best and only friend for most of my life. She chooses to believe that I was negligent in sending her across the world. I was negligent because of my ignorance about international travel and for not arranging for her to be met at the airport or educating her about what she was about to experience. However, considering my background and the limitations of my own coming of age, I did what I thought best and it proved to be correct in ways she has not realized and therefore will not acknowledge.

At that time, Bob left his position with A Thousand Trails and started a property-management business all the way across Lake Washington in Bellevue's upscale business district. Bob had to take the ferry across Puget Sound, get a car parked in a garage downtown, and then make the morning commute across the Evergreen Point Bridge to his office. It was a heroic endeavor and the new company was beginning to prove viable. I realized that if I supported his endeavors and we focused on him, we'd all benefit greatly. I closed up the studio and was ready to get behind my husband's endeavors one hundred percent. We packed up our family and made the move across the sound into the city, where we tried on a traditional Jewish life.

Antithetical to our rural situation on the island, we settled on a busy city street. We found a charming house right next door to the rabbi and his, wife Annie. Our children played together and went to the Jewish Day School. I continued to weave and study. I loved making special Sabbath meals each week. Although the congregation was conservative, we leaned toward orthodoxy. Following as many regulative principals as I could, I made all the Sabbath meals in advance. We all went to the Saturday morning synagogue service and, for a while, I enjoyed sanctified time and our family had a bit of structured cohesion.

As usual, however, I began to see our experience as a placebo. The Jewish community we belonged to was made up of bright, well-educated and well-positioned professionals who had gone to the right schools and had a good deal of pride in their accomplishments. I did not fit in; nor did I want to. Once again I began to feel alienated and dissatisfied. Neti-neti. Once I saw the false view or felt out of sync with my yet-unrealized person-hood, I could no longer participate. My foray into Judaism left me cold and dispirited. The Saturday morning synagogue services no longer fed my soul. While Bob began to amass the money he always dreamed about, I prayed for guidance. He was satisfied with his life, and I, as usual, was not.

Although we still lived next door to the rabbi and his family, I left synagogue life behind and, once again, found myself sitting in the void of not knowing. I dug deeply. I wanted to know what preceded Judaism. I had a feeling, which I could not ignore.

NATURE CALLS

Some think of myth as a narrative without logical circumstance and, therefore, they discount its validity for depicting actual events. Yet, myth is the language of the soul and best describes that which cannot be understood analytically or rationally.

After my foray into Judaism, I studied feminist literature. Sylvia Brinton Perera's book, *The Descent to the Goddess: A Way of Initiation for Women,* was an essential piece of my puzzle. In her book she tells of Inanna, the Sumerian Queen of Heaven, who descends to the depths of hell leaving a bit of herself behind at each level. Archaeological findings prove that goddess worship flourished for thousands of years before the arrival of Abraham, the first prophet of the misogynistic male deity Yahweh.

I was beginning to understand something about the nature of the sacrifices a woman might make for her children and her husband. I had happened onto pertinent and potent information that encouraged me to delve deeper into the ancient religions.

I read books on the agrarian societies that Old Testament Abraham fought to destroy. The *Jewish Encyclopedia* refers to the writing of Chearchus of Soli who wrote extensively around 320 BCE. He was a disciple of Aristotle and his enthusiasm for Eastern culture fueled his writing and studies. His view was that pre-Judaic Hebrews were descendants of Indian Vedic philosophers. I also realized that the beginning of Jewish history coincided with the beginning of the Kaliyuga. I then realized how the coming of the patriarchs turned the age toward a misogynistic worldview.

The Vedas teach us that human civilization degenerates spiritually during the Kali Yuga. The Kali Yuga is referred to as the Dark Age because at this time people suffer from impersonalism and lead compromised lives full of quarrel and hypocrisy. I was romantic in my view of the goddess worshiping cultures believing that matriarchal societies were relatively peaceful and that the goddess worshiping civilizations of ancient Babylon, Syria and Palestine— amongst other Middle Eastern regions—were the agricultural communities that Abraham tried to destroy. I imagined that these goddess-centered communities celebrated the seasons with reverence for what this good earth yields. I believed that they held feminine energy in high esteem. And so did I. I was being born again and nature was my refuge.

HORSES

Jungian Analyst James Hillman describes in his best-selling book, *The Soul's Code,* how we might carry the destiny for a child not yet born. I feel that much of my early life was directed for the sake of my second son, Jeremy, who went on to become a world-famous classical horse trainer. I share this information not to brag about my child's accomplishments or his fame, because all my children have realized success on the material plane. (After all, I am a Jewish mother.) My karma, my life, and my destiny have been intricately and intimately interwoven with my offspring, as is every mother's destiny.

In Vaishnava tradition, or the culture of Krishna, the horse in the form of the incarnation Hayagriva represents the battle of wisdom and knowledge against darker demonic forces. Hayagriva is depicted as a white horse with a humanoid body. As the *Rig Veda,* the earliest extant literature, extolls the superior stealthy qualities of the equine species:

"Slight us not Varuna, Aryaman, or Mitra, Rbhuksan, Indra, Āyu, or the Maruts,

When we declare amid the congregation the virtues of the strong Steed, God-descended."

The alluring smell of hay, manure and sweat coupled with grooming brushes and the equine creature's voluminous soft eyes created a compelling world where I was able to resurrect myself in a wholly new way.

While still living on a busy street in Seattle, our income increased sufficiently and I began to fulfill a childhood dream by taking riding lessons. This pull into the equestrian world supported my studies of the Goddess religions. Taken out of my mind and into my body on rainy afternoons in a large horse barn, with women who didn't care what schools I went to or who I knew or how I made a living, was the medicine I needed. No longer just dreaming of trail rides and the earthy aroma of hay and manure, I realized a dream for Jeremy and myself.

Jeremy, then twelve, had an early-morning paper route and became one of a group of boys who felt that the neighborhood streets were their playground. One day I received a phone call from the local Safeway market. "Hello, Mrs.___, we caught your son Jeremy stealing cigarettes from our store." I was aghast, thinking him angelic and incapable of any wrong. The manager went on to say, "If you punish him appropriately we will not bring charges."

Pondering the situation and knowing that Jeremy's natural horse-whispering talents should be realized, I considered a different kind of punishment. At that time, my knowledge of horses was quite slim and I was not able to recognize a talented, well-trained horse from a green one. Late that afternoon, Jeremy and I took the ferry across Puget Sound to Indianola, where we found a homely pony named Daisy. Many children had ridden this poor creature for "gaming." She was sour, old, and ugly. Jeremy said, "Let's buy her, Mom."

So, for five hundred dollars, including all tack, Daisy was transported to the barn where I was learning to ride. No longer interested in anything else, Jeremy soon turned that pony into a happy creature who won ribbons at the 4H horse shows. His career was launched.

Also at that barn I met Vicki Powers, an inspiring naturalist who raised Chihuahuas. Now you might be wondering how a horse and a Chihuahua can change a fate or shape a story. Or, how I could be writing a spiritual memoir filled with scriptural references and then tell animal stories. Yet, I need to share that at this juncture magical creatures began to appear in my life, beginning with a puppy.

With my focus on nature and Jeremy's love for horses, the decision to move was reasonable to me and Bob was amenable. We took the kids out of the Jewish day school and changed our perspective entirely.

This abrupt move was hard for our youngest, Rachel, who was very happy with her life as it was. In many ways we all sacrificed for Jeremy's career. I found a property high on Hollywood Hill in Woodinville that would accommodate horses and, once again, allow us a somewhat rural lifestyle. The antiquated equestrian property, which we eventually renovated, had views of Seattle's Space Needle and also the Cascade Mountains to the rear.

The well-situated Hollywood Hill property would be our last residence together as a family. Remodeling and moving kept Bob and me from facing the inevitable breech that would soon come. Our home in Woodinville was lovely. We had an extensive garden and a flowing driveway lined with poppies, daffodils and tulips. I designed a small pond and surrounded it with rose quartz. It appeared idyllic but it wasn't. Everyone, including me, had an agenda. We were without family cohesion.

Every Sunday morning my mother would call for our usual "everything is wonderful" conversation. I would tell her only good things about the marriage, the children and Bob's career. Prior to cell phones, we had a phone in the barn near the doorway. One Sunday morning while I was doing barn chores, my mother called, asking her usual question, "How's everything?" At that moment, as I stood in the doorway, looking back at the house and the picturesque landscape, everything seemed to disintegrate. Without any warning, my life went from denial to trial.

I replied, "Nothing is as it seems, no one is really happy, the marriage is horrible, and I am miserable." My mom replied, "Donna, you come from a family with a lot of mental illness; perhaps it's time you sought help." My mom's remedy was to take a pill and go back to sleep, but I couldn't pretend any longer.

We had made our last move. There was no place else to hide and nothing else we could do to keep the marriage alive. It wasn't just my spiritual inclinations. It seemed to me that Bob's character decreased as his income increased. Somehow

Bob couldn't treat me with respect and kindness in front of the children which was very important to me. I didn't want them to grow up in an insensitive environment like I had. When Bob was a star basketball player in high school and college, his strategy was to keep everyone at a distance. That strategy, whether conscious or not, was his mode of being within the family by keeping us apart from each other. I felt like an incidental that he considered an eccentric novelty while being treated without the loving-respect and emotional protection that a wife dearly desires.

I had threatened Bob with divorce so many times along the way that he was deaf to my threats. Yet, I knew that the day would come when I would no longer be able to continue to suffer the emptiness. I tried the best I could with what I had, living most of those years isolated from emotional warmth not unlike my family of origin.

I remember our last Thanksgiving; Jill, Jeremy and Adam were on their own and came back to Woodinville to share the Holiday with Bob, Rachel and me. Along with a few friends, we sat around a large dining table in our designer home. I realized that the conversations were mean-spirited and the humor was not nurturing, but always at the expense of someone else. My children vied for who could be the most quick-witted, sarcastic and cynical. I felt like Bob enjoyed seeing me ground down by the acrimonious attitudes he fostered. How could I continue in that spiritually polluted and emotionally draining environment?

BUDDHISM *
IMPERSONALISM

I read Phillip Kapleau's *Three Pillars of Zen* when I was in my late twenties. From that time until not long ago, I was keen to learn as much as possible about Buddhist practice and philosophy. Shortly before the dissolution of my marriage, through my association with the owner of the Woodinville Thai Restaurant, I had the opportunity to learn something about Theravada Buddhism and its mindfulness practices. Narlamon was a disciple of Ajahn Tong—the head meditation master in the northern province of Thailand and teacher to the royal family.

I enjoyed visiting with Narlamon in her restaurant. I valued the friendship she offered and, of course, I also enjoyed the mindfully presented classic Thai meals that she and her husband lovingly prepared each day. She knew I was interested in Buddhism and the Thai culture because of my appreciation of the Buddhist statues and photos that adorned the restaurant walls. Narlamon was also delighted to share her enthusiasm for the Vipassana retreats that the emissaries of Ajahn Tong led when they were in the U.S.

A season or two passed before Kate and her husband arrived in Woodinville from their South American teaching tour. Kate was an American woman in her late thirties, and Thanat, in his early to mid-fifties, was Chinese. When meeting them both, it was Thanat's broad smile and charming manner that put me at ease. They told me the upcoming retreat would be held at the nearby home of another of Ajahn Tong's adherents.

I was in a new culture and strange territory and eager to learn everything I could. Thanat then told me that I must plan to attend the retreat for two weeks. Up until that time, I had never been away from Bob and Rachel for any significant length of time. I replied that I could come for a long weekend, perhaps, but certainly not two weeks.

Thanat, with his broad grin and easy manner, began to tell me why two weeks would be necessary for success. He used the analogy of an airplane taking off for a long flight. He said the plane would go through a layer of turbulence, caused by low clouds, before it could attain cruising altitude and level off. I sat in the restaurant booth, attentively listening to their description of what might come. After the initial conversation and a few jokes, they invited me to their home in Everett, Washington for an introduction to Vipassana meditation practice.

Not yet agreeing to the two weeks, I did agree to visit them in Everett. Later that week when I met with them, Thanat began to tell me more about the nature of mind exercises we would be using. He explained how I had to train my mind to recognize attachments and aversions that ultimately are the causes of suffering.

The tool I would use through disciplined practice would be the sword of awareness. This technique would cut through disturbances by developing my ability to recognize thoughts and feelings as they arose. He further explained to me how I would learn to follow my breath, noting the rising and falling of my abdomen or chest, as I breathed in and breathed out. Staying present, I would silently repeat, "rising, falling, sitting," and when my mind would wander or when any thought or feeling would come, I would simply say, "thinking, thinking, thinking," repeating the word three times, acknowledging that thoughts or feelings arise, prevail, and dissipate.

He adamantly told me, "Donna, never follow the thoughts; cut them with the sword of awareness right away. He went on, using anger as an example: " Just acknowledge: anger, anger, anger...do not elaborate, justify or continue thinking." He again emphasized, "Do not follow when the feeling arises; just recognize it and come right back to your breath: rising, falling, sitting."

I was to begin simply enough with a five-minute seated practice, followed by a five-minute walking practice. The walking practice had numerous stages. During stage one, I was to acknowledge standing and then lifting my foot, moving my foot forward and placing my foot on the ground: right goes thus, left goes thus. As I became more experienced, the level of acknowledgment would increase, eventually to heel up, lifting, moving placing, heel down. The more accurate I could become, the more awareness I would develop, and the further I would progress on the path of mindfulness.

Soon enough it was time for the retreat to begin. Neither Bob nor Rachel showed any interest in what I was about to do; nor did they show any concern for my leaving. So, two weeks of steady mindfulness practice lay ahead. The morning I was to meet Thanat, Kate, and Narlamon at the restaurant, Bob did drive me down the hill away from our home. I was to wear only white clothing for the entire two weeks and told not to bring any books or diversions.

I remember meeting a gray van in the parking lot of the Woodinville Thai Restaurant. I was somewhat nervous, realizing that I was about to leave my known world and enter into a foreign culture with people I hardly knew. Up until that time, nothing I did had any noticeable effect on my disposition.

Narlamon waved good-bye as Thanat, Kate, and I drove away. We arrived at a suburban home on a cul-de-sac. I was surprised that I would be spending two weeks at this seemingly bland American house. With an open mind I went up the front steps with Kate and Thanat and knocked gently on the door. A short, pudgy Thai woman greeted us with a large welcoming smile.

Coming into the foyer, I immediately sensed I was entering into a foreign land. In the sparsely furnished living room was a golden altar that held a big Buddha who presided over many pictures of other Buddhist deities and smaller statues. There were no chairs or other tables in the room. In the dining room, a stuffed toy monkey with a Mexican sombrero hung on the wall. That duly noted, I realized my powers of observation were already well engaged and something different was afoot!

Thanat then introduced me to our hostess, Supawadee. After greeting us at the door, she immediately went into the kitchen to finish luncheon preparations for her guests. I was just one of a few people she would be looking after while we practiced mindfulness under Thanat and Kate's supervision.

Still holding my suitcase, I watched as Supawadee squatted over a bamboo mat on her kitchen floor peeling the luncheon vegetables. When she noticed me standing in the doorway of the kitchen, she laid down her utensils and told me to follow her through a door that led out to the garage. The garage was stocked with enough packaged-food supplies to last until the end of time as well as a dining table and its many chairs.

Supawadee pointed to a barely noticeable crawl space, telling me that my bedroom would be on the other side of that wall through the small entrance way. To say I was suspicious and unbelieving would not do justice to my reaction. Only three or four feet high, the passageway did not invite me to investigate further. Puzzled, I looked at her and thought perhaps I was about to be kidnapped and sequestered in an underground cave. Seeing my reaction, Supawadee opened the door and pointed down the steep stairway that led to a dimly lit recreation room. I knew that neither Bob nor anyone else would check on my whereabouts for some time. So, if something were awry my absence would go unnoticed.

Something about the lack of concern anyone had for me made me drop to my knees and creep through the strange opening. Once on the ground floor, I was in a separate environment with two normal sheet rocked bedrooms with windows to the outside. However, Supawadee and her American husband, who worked as an engineer at Boeing, had carved additional rooms into the hillside. These were windowless cave-like dwellings. As I was the first guest to arrive, I chose a carpeted bedroom with two windows.

Following Watt (Temple) Chom Tong's schedule, we were to awaken a little before 4:00 a.m. to practice one round of sitting and one round of walking meditation before the 6:00 a.m. breakfast. Each session would last fifty-five minutes. Supawadee with her wonderful sense of humor rapidly became an ally. She would serve after hour snacks and encourage a few of us to sit with her long after we should have retired. We were meant to socialize very little, staying mindful each moment. However, Thanat also had a lenient point of view about remaining silent. He expressed it this way: "You have six sense doors: seeing, touching, tasting, feeling, smelling and mind. If you close one door too tightly, you will force another to open. Therefore, speak if you must but use discretion."

With breakfast at 6:00 a.m., lunch was served at 11:30 a.m. Again adhering to the mother temple's schedule, we were not supposed to take any other nourishment after lunch. Strangely, though, we could eat ice cream or other snack foods that were not considered a meal. Between breakfast and lunch we practiced two more rounds of walking and sitting meditation. After luncheon we met privately with Kate and Thanat in front of the living room altar. With hands in prayer position in front of our heart we took refuge in the Buddha, the dharma, and the sangha by kneeling down and touching our forehead to the floor three times. Afterward Kate and Thanat proceeded to ask questions concerning our practices, hoping we would begin to understand the importance of knowing impermanence and the causes of suffering.

We were discouraged from going outside where any distraction could potentially cause our plane to crash! Proceeding this way, I climbed the yannas, or pathway to realizations. For instance, the day before concluding the retreat, a loving feeling came over me. Instead of acknowledging the feeling, I projected it onto Bob, still hoping for the unrealizable happy marriage. Disobeying the rules, I tried to reach Bob by phone, wanting to express my appreciation. But he ignored the call, as he often did.

The hope-filled bubble burst and I had a dizzy feeling as my mind reeled in circles and then anger arose. I had a first-class lesson in the principle of causality, a basic teaching in all the Buddhist schools. The retreat ended with a small ceremony, hugs were exchanged, and I went back to my home high on Hollywood Hill in Woodinville, Washington. My experience was successful because I was still able to follow my breath in my sleep while acknowledging: sleeping, sleeping, sleeping.

Later that year I was invited to go to the mother temple in Thailand. I didn't want to go. Somehow, I knew that trip would be the end of my life as it was. Even though I was miserable, I still had hope for our marriage and family life. I asked Bob and Rachel how they felt about my leaving for six weeks, which again seemed impossibly long. Both father and daughter looked at me unresponsively. As I saw them, the choices I had were either to stay home and endure or be open to what life was offering. So, on a cold, snowy day in February of 1997, a dejected me took a hired shuttle to the airport.

Once in Thailand under the guidance of Ajahn Tong, I arose at 4:00 a.m. and began the steady mindfulness practice of walking and sitting meditation. This time I found that sitting for fifty-five minutes in an upright position without support was difficult. I was sure that Vipassana was an exit plan from misery; therefore, I needed to become an accomplished meditator. After all, the Buddha taught that there's nothing but suffering and, to date, that had been my life experience.

Sitting in my little room at the Watt, I decided to press my back against the wall and stuff socks behind me to add pressure where I hurt. I knew if my meditation would ever leave the realm of acknowledging the pain, I would have to build strength. I would need support, both emotionally and physically. I knew my body was a reflection of my disintegrating life. I was not yet fifty years old and I was at the start of my reformation.

The Sanskrit word tapa, among other meanings, also implies austere self-disciplines as a means to realize the real self. The *Chandogya Upanishad* further offers that those who engage in tapas, that is austerities, and self-examination, will succeed in their pursuit of actual realization. The *Upanishads* embrace the nature of reality and describe a path to liberation. I needed practices that distanced me from the pain I felt while coming to terms with my disillusionment. Therefore, Buddhism and its view of the world as impersonal suited me.

"The living entity, while executing devotional service or transcendental rituals after many, many births, may actually become situated in the pure transcendental knowledge that the Supreme Personality of Godhead is the ultimate goal of spiritual realization. At the beginning of spiritual realization, while one is trying to give up one's attachment to materialism, there is some leaning toward impersonalism, but when one is further advanced he can understand that there are activities in the spiritual life and that these activities constitute devotional service. Realizing this, he/she becomes attached to the Supreme Personality of Godhead and surrenders to Him. At such

time, one can understand that Lord Sri Krsna's mercy is everything.
(B-g.7.19)

Though I was on the yoga ladder, I still had quite a way to go before I came to realize Krishna's Mercy.

THE WATT

The Watt (Phradhatu Sri Chom Tong Voravihara) an hour north of Chaing Mai, is referred to as The Holy Relic Monastery on the Glorious Golden Hill. Now a historic site, it is highly revered because of the sacred Buddha relic that is enshrined there. Legend has it that the Lord Buddha came to teach the people on a hill very near to the monastery.

I was fortunate to be a student of the head abbot, Ajahn Tong. I well remember our first interview. At the end of day one I was taken to his chambers where an interpreter seated between Ajahn Tong and me helped us communicate. Ajahn Tong asked me how I was doing and I didn't hesitate to tell him that I felt sad. He was happy to hear this and replied, "That is very good, because you are like an oxen who has been free in the field, and now you have been brought in and tethered. When you give up the struggle you will begin in earnest."

I had my own little meditation hut, a kuti. It was luxurious with its own bathroom and shower. Around the perimeter of the kuti I could practice walking meditation. Mornings would begin with the monks chanting in Pali, the sacred language of

Theravada Buddhism. Their melodious voices and the steady rhythm comforted me as I woke to a new day so far from home. At the end of the day I would practice on the temple rooftop, watching the sun go down and the monks scurrying about to get the day's chores finished.

A month passed and I became restless and, against the advice of Ajahn Tong, I decided to leave the Watt. When I told Ajahn Tong I would be leaving, he encouraged me to stay and become a teacher. When I declined, he said: "It is not the time for you to go; you will see nothing but suffering." I didn't realize that he was referring to my level of practice. I just thought that was the Buddhist view of life outside the temple.

Again, something within prodded me on. Neti-neti. Walking away from Watt Chom Tong, just outside the temple gates on the broad sidewalk toward the main road, I saw a three-legged dog dying a painful death.

When I phoned Bob from the stopover in Singapore and told him of my arrival time in Seattle, he told me to take a cab home. I knew nothing had changed. Acknowledging sadness, I arrived back in the States further alienated from my grown children and my husband's comfortable materialism.

I couldn't make sense of my life. The constant mindfulness practice turned me into a robotic observation machine. Feeling outside myself, I tried a few therapeutic modalities to help me integrate back into Western culture but nothing worked. I continued to meditate in the Thai style, twice each day. Setting my cushion on the floor by the bedroom window, looking out over the yard, toward Seattle, my mood was as gray, damp, and foggy as the weather.

When I heard Bob come up the stairs, I would acknowledge either sadness or anger. I thought the meditation practice would see me through to the end of my days. I couldn't foresee what was to come.

THE TURNING POINT *
HATHA-YOGA

I began to practice Hatha-yoga when I was a teenager. Those were the days of gentle yoga done at a slow pace, meant to nourish the soul while keeping the back flexible and raising one's kundalini—vital energy.

Classes were held in churches or other nonprofit environments. Much later, in the mid-nineties, on the east side of Seattle, Hatha-yoga studios were beginning to open in unusual places. The Iyengar studio was located in a strip mall and the Bikram studio was situated in a warehouse.

Not able to get into a groove after returning from the Watt, I looked for a yoga class and chose to attend the Bikram studio for its convenience. When I called to inquire, I was told to bring a water bottle and towel and just show up, which I did the following morning.

I immediately took to the practice. Every asana was challenging but doable. Ninety minutes of focused physical activity that required internal awareness was what I needed and my attitude changed immediately after the first class. I thought the Hatha-yoga and Vipassana meditation would allow me to tolerate my relationship with my husband and cope with the difficult circumstances of my marriage. Though disheartened by my lengthy stay in Thailand and its resultant disengagement, I still believed the road to liberation was impersonal. Buddhist philosophy was still appealing, and the Hatha-yoga practice fortified me.

THE MUSE *
A FRESH START

Shedding my skin on Seattle's streets, I pursued the muse.
Wily musicians laid down their tracks while tunes lingered
in hallways and doorways and under eaves and archways.
I made my way down 2nd Avenue southward past Lenora.
Heading down Pine, I heard a clarinet and I pursued the
muse. The Prayers born in my heart on that very day traveled
well and far... taken from my diary 1997

Inspiration is the beginning of self-inquiry. It is also the drawing in of one's breath. In need of inspiration, I was moved outward by my Hatha-yoga practice. I began to roam Seattle's city streets, looking for something beyond the ordinary.

Walking along the perimeter of the famous Pike Place Market, I noticed Morgan on the corner of Pike and Pine. He was wearing a long tweed coat and an Irish cap, with his clarinet pointed upward toward the green Seattle street sign. He appeared to me as The Fool in the Rider-Waite tarot deck. Mesmerized by his archetypal appearance, I froze as people rushed past.

I was ready for a mythical journey and hungry for the connection that would take me out of my belittling marriage and unhappy family situation. I knew there was a kind of happiness that was not dependent on how much I had or who I knew or where I worked or any other material circumstance.

Seattle's wealth steadily grew during the 1990s. The city was booming. Microsoft had made its enormous campus across Lake Washington on Seattle's east side. Amazon's offices had moved into Freemont. Starbucks located its corporate office in Pioneer Square. High-end shopping proliferated. Traffic became unbearable. Commerce was unending. I wanted out.

It is no wonder that the image of a street musician playing in Seattle's rain caught my attention in such a profound way. I hated the materialistic culture. Leaving one's family is part of what Joseph Campbell titled *The Heroes Journey.* I had to break away from all that was familiar and acceptable. Bikram's "HAVE NO FEAR! Just do my yoga, and you will become you!" seemed to be working on me. I had a vague uneasiness under my skin that kept me on the lookout for signs and situations, omens and predilections. Morgan's hat was slightly tilted, his overcoat too big, and his clarinet case open. The incongruity of people rushing past stopped me in my tracks.

After two years of consistent Hatha-yoga practice, I was on the lookout for meaningful work. I enjoyed going downtown and photographing the musicians who worked the corners of Seattle's busy streets. Introducing myself to Morgan, the clarinet player, I began to learn about the street culture.

While downtown I had frequent conversations with the low-income folks who sold the Real Change Homeless Empowerment Project newspapers on designated spots throughout the city. I walked the streets near Pike Place Market, comforted by the barking sea gulls that dove for leftovers and the mystical sound of the foghorns as the ferries crossed Puget Sound. While in some corner, under a doorway, in an archway, street music wove its way into the fabric of Seattle's unique culture.

One day while sitting in Seattle's Best Coffee Shop I read an article by Timothy Harris, the founding editor of the *Real Change* paper. Tim was looking to refurbish a space that would allow low-income and homeless artists to produce work without the high cost of a studio rental. He needed a photographer and director for the gallery. I knew I would be good at both positions.

I was excited by the prospect of something meaningful to do and immediately went up to 2nd Avenue to find Tim. My enthusiasm was well received and he gave me the go-ahead for both positions. I was ecstatic.

A few days later, I met Roberto at the door of what would soon be the gallery. His handsome face and panache took my breath away. He was a street-smart, savvy guy who knew a good opportunity when he saw one. Recently clean and sober from a lifetime of alcohol and drug abuse, Roberto was looking for a way to further himself. Selling his paintings put a few necessary dollars in his pockets. He had heard about the gallery and workshop space and was hoping for an environment where he could flourish in his newly found sobriety.

We both approached the door from opposite directions—I from the south and he from the north. As he was walking toward the door, I observed him as a strikingly tall man in a motorcycle jacket and a green turtleneck. As he got closer, I saw a well-chiseled face with a long gray ponytail. He looked like a member of an Italian noble family, with deep-set blue eyes, high cheekbones, and a well-defined patrician nose. In this downtown neighborhood of crack dealers and mendicants, I was far from home. Roberto appeared to represent all the freedom I aspired to have.

With Roberto rolling up his sleeves alongside me, we spent one month refurbishing the building and hauling trash to the dump. In between cleaning and hauling we walked the city streets, deep in conversation. I learned a lot about Seattle's avant-garde artists and the drug culture. Astute about the street scene, Robert became my sergeant-at-arms as people began to roll into the gallery hoping for a working space.

Robert Francis Valenza, calling himself Roberto for the gusto, sorted the people as they came to the door. Those whom he believed to be still on drugs or alcohol were not allowed to participate. Mental illness was common but acceptable. We had a fair number of participants with severe personality disorders. After we established the rules and hung our first show, we had a grand opening complete with representation from the mayor's office and a bit of press coverage.

I was Wendy to the Lost Boys. I listened, counseled, applauded, encouraged and befriended everyone who came into the gallery. It was a glorious time for me. I loved the job and began to see how happiness is not contingent on income or occupation.

A few women who frequented the gallery and lived below it in a womens' shelter invited me to dinner one night. Sitting at their round table, enjoying the camaraderie, I realized that these women were happier than I. That was the night I began to cut my ties to the wealth-driven suburbs.

Every morning before coming across the bridge into the city from the eastside, I would clean out my house and load my truck with every superfluous belonging we had. Eventually I even gave away my canvases and brushes, paints and fixatives. Nothing was too dear or precious. All the while I worked downtown at the gallery, I continued to cross the bridge back over Lake Washington to attend yoga classes in Kirkland, and then back home to life with Bob.

Roberto was impressed with my resolve. He had lived in India and Nepal for a number of years and thought of himself as a sadhu. And, in all truth, with his hair piled in a topknot on the top of his head, he was unmistakably unusual.

GOOD-BYE

Later, when I realized the pain I caused when I left Bob and Rachel, each beat of my heart slowed to an anguished crawl. My throat closed up so tightly that every breath was an unwelcome reminder of what would never be. I was strangled by my inability to do any more for any of them. Like a small bird flying across an immense ocean, I searched for a landing place. I continuously prayed that I would never cause another human being the suffering that Bob endured when I finally had the strength and courage to go.

I knew my family would never fully understand my situation. The twenty-five-year illusion of happiness I gave my parents was dispelled the instant everyone realized I was serious and would not return. I was abandoned, disowned as well as disinherited by my parents as a result of Bob's persuasion and his urgent need to keep his province protected. Still believing that my worth was in my marriage, my mother and father did as Bob insisted. They wrote me out of their lives and out of their will.

I was exhausted by the magnitude of my grief. I walked away from all things familiar. Needing time and space, I took a little road trip along the scenic Olympic Peninsula. Driving along the edge of the Hood Canal, my first sigh and reflective moments were on a rocky slope. There, I felt relief seeing the way the sky met the water and the water kissed the shore. I watched children play. Boys approached one another. A little girl in pink overalls climbed carefully up a rocky ledge. I remember thinking that children seek each other and, somewhere in time, there is a landscape where I belong. Someday I would find that place. But then, the winter's chill froze my heart and I couldn't imagine spring's thaw.

Swimming the ocean of samsara—the repetitious cycle of birth and rebirth—with nothing but family discord, I was on Arjuna's battlefield the opening scene in the Song of God, the *Bhagavad-gita*. My marriage was disparaged and I had pretended long enough. I did everything I could to create a loving and kind family, yet to no avail. Everyone was in it for himself or herself. The plaintive echo of Morgan's clarinet had awakened me. I heard it as the shankha, one of the many conch shells blown at the onset of the Kurukshetra War that occurred many millennia ago just outside Delhi.

It was time for me to be decisive. Leaving was traumatic but necessary. I could not delay any longer, even if it meant being homeless and joining the many who lived downtown in Seattle's shelters and missions. I had to make a stand. I knew I had to leave the comfort of my home. Buddhist practice helped me loosen my grasp. I needed to have faith in the omens as I saw them.

THE DIVORCE

I spent the four seasons of my epic divorce in a tiny second-floor apartment above the dumpsters, behind the coffee shop next to Seattle's very first Bikram studio. It was a noisy, back-alley neighborhood. Anxious over my limited finances and not knowing the future, I chain-smoked Marlborough Lights. However, during that time I learned an important lesson. It's not my will but God's will that will be done and God loves those who help themselves.

I found a lucrative job photographing Indonesian artwork and preparing the digital images for the web and print. At that time my skills with digital imaging, which I had learned toward the end of the marriage, were valuable.

Between yoga classes, I sat in the corner of my apartment in an old English armchair, smoking those god-awful cigarettes, blowing the smoke out the window and watching it dissipate in Seattle's perpetual dark-winter dampness. Getting ready for class, I bathed to remove the stench and then went down the old building's stairs and up the adjacent metal stairs to Kathy and Kevin Cooke's premier hot-yoga studio. The yoga kept me strong-minded and determined. Even though I was nauseous from the cigarettes, I attended class every day. When I wasn't smoking I was chewing my lip. Yet, I knew I was right to reclaim my life and, no matter how long the rectification would take, I had no choice.

The divorce took a full year because my husband was beside himself with grief and disbelief, "even though I told him to take heed of my numinous illuminations!" It wasn't losing me that caused him so much angst. It was the idea that he would have to split the holdings. After a year of angst and nail-biting, lip-chewing anxiety, the divorce was finalized just in time for me to attend Bikram's last yoga training of the twentieth century. All events synchronized nicely. With a car packed and a new life ahead, I put out my last cigarette and was on my way to Beverly Hills.

YOGA TRAINING

My traveling companion, Roberto Valenza (1943-2010)
was a poet and early member of Seattle's Red Sky Poetry
Theatre. Much of his early work is now archived at the
University of Washington.

The year I spent overlooking the dumpsters in the little Green Lake apartment, working on my large computer screen digitizing photos for the Indonesian business, I also contacted a company in Orange County that restored Airstream trailers for Hollywood movie sets. They had a twenty-four-foot, 1954 Airstream they were willing to restore for me. So, I traded my economical Volkswagen bug for a gas-guzzling beast that would eventually pull the trailer.

Following the coastline from Washington State, we drove a jam-packed white Chevy Suburban to Los Angeles. Both Roberto and I were at once high on leaving our past behind and anxious about what might come our way. Through the miraculous Internet I also managed to find a cute apartment to sublet in Brentwood, right near the 405 freeway and Sunset Boulevard. Roberto was skeptical about the deal and sure that the sublet was a rip-off and would not be waiting for us on arrival. I found the landlord on a rental site intended for students of The University of California, Los Angeles, UCLA. Though I was not a student of UCLA, the landlord rented us the apartment. Because I had come with Roberto to the training, Bikram's own student housing was not appropriate.

The training required me to do two, ninety-minute hot yoga classes each day, morning and evening, five days each week and one class on Saturday. We were given Sunday to catch up on shopping, cooking and laundry. The middle part of the day was spent mostly with Bikram and his senior teachers learning the intricacies of teaching—namely, the dialog: Bikram's scripted teaching method.

We spent some evenings listening to outrageous tales of Bikram's early Hollywood escapades but no matter how I might have been inconvenienced or kept up way beyond my bedtime, I'll always be respectful and appreciative of what he taught me. Regardless of what my circumstances were, after becoming a practitioner and teacher, the yoga kept me strong in the face of adversity. Bikram regularly said, "If you let anyone steal your peace you are the loser."

Being in Beverly Hills for nine weeks and practicing with Bikram's star-studded students was exceedingly strenuous and, at the same time, fun. We graduated just before Christmas 1999 and I was able to teach in the Beverly Hills studio right away.

My first class had many of Bikram's senior teachers in it as well as many of his Hollywood Illuminati, such as Lainie Kazan and Martin Sheen's wife, Janet. I tripped over my

tongue all the way through my first teaching experience but it was an excellent way to launch.

Just before the turn of the century, sixty-four bright, shiny faces graduated from the training. It was a big deal. The editor of the yoga journal gave a talk. Amrit Desai, founder of the Kripalu yoga center in Lenox, Massachusetts also delivered a speech. I believe our graduation was the first of its size ever in the Western yoga community.

Whether it was right or wrong, Bikram created a business of Hatha-yoga and set an example that is now a business model for yoga studios worldwide. Bikram was always kind to me. He discouraged me from opening a studio in calamity-prone Topanga Canyon, invited me to his home, and treated me with respect.

Though I paid the high price that the training cost, it gave me a means of support, right livelihood, self-respect and good health. These benefits are priceless; the sequence is a miracle, and I will always be fond of Bikram Choudhury.

The commitment to practice yoga, the commitment to teach, the commitment to just show up day after day with a happy, smiling face is a rewarding discipline. Doing Bikram's sequence acts as a reset button. It flushes away stagnant energy while increasing overall health and, no matter who is in the yoga room, it is my job to enter the teaching arena with a happy, smiling face and be positive and encouraging each and every moment.

INTO THE FUTURE

I knew that the silver Airstream would take us into the future. As such, I thought of it as a time machine and time was on our side. The trailer's restoration coincided with the end of the nine-week training. We picked up the vessel in Orange County shortly after New Year's. I had some experience towing a trailer because I transported Jeremy's horses before he was old enough to drive the truck and trailer himself.

We stayed at an RV park near Mission Beach, where we spent our first few days getting familiar with the Airstream's setup. I had good friends who lived nearby and shared our enthusiasm for the pending odyssey. When it was time to go, they sent us off with well wishes and heartfelt hugs.

Our first stop with the Airstream was in Ajo, Arizona. Upon arrival we did the usual things required. But, after settling in, I found it impossible to relax. I was a newly released prisoner with post-traumatic stress disorder that was ready to take me down at any time. To say I was clueless would be a compliment.

An RV park is primarily for retirees and vacationers. I was neither. I've never been a pleasure seeker nor could I understand why not. I just knew that I hated to waste time. There was something I needed to do and something I needed to know and that something drove me every single day. I wanted a genuinely satisfying life. I wanted knowledge of the SOURCE OF EVERYTHING. I wanted the ABSOLUTE TRUTH. But I had no idea of how to go about reaching such a glorious conclusion. I still had miles to go, both figuratively and literally. When I fell short, I would become misanthropic.

I quickly saw the downside of being on the road in Kerouac fashion with Roberto, a neo-beatnik, hippy person whose goal in life was to do as little work as possible and just slide by. How was I to know what I was facing? I had little life experience beyond a sheltered marriage. I was still enamored of beatnik jargon and hippy clichés. I wanted the peace, love and happiness that the sixties and seventies promised, but that time had already passed.

It was the winter of 2000 and the system did not collapse, as had been predicted with the turning of the century, Y2K. I longed to be more advanced, more experienced and wiser than I was. I knew that the qualities I desired were within but, not knowing how to attain them, I looked outward. Newly divorced, never on my own, not knowing what the future held, I was constantly on edge.

Once settled in the RV Park and after a short bike ride to check out the small town, I returned to the Airstream. In contrast to this dry little mining town, I began to think back on my most recent time in Encinitas, California when Roberto and I visited the Self-Realization Fellowship on the cliffs above the sea. Not only was I born on the anniversary of the Holocaust, I was also blessed with similar planetary aspects to Paramahansa Yogananda.

That day in Ajo, Arizona, my memories took me to the church of waves. I recalled the euphoric feelings I had under the cliffs in Encinitas and how I ran along the shore as the seagulls scattered and dispersed airborne blessings. I remembered seeing the surfers, so far off the coast, looking like shamans dancing out on the edge where the air meets the sea. I noted the young, lithe little bodies in rubber suits that glided between sea and sky like they were like tightrope walkers on a thin thread of white foam. In my dreamlike state I lost track of time and all too soon the harsh desert wind brought me back to my present-moment anxieties in Ajo, Arizona.

The next morning I probed deeply into the corners of my discomforts. I expected more from myself but there was a raging war inside me. I projected this onto the environment. Finding the desert inhospitable, I contemplated driving two hundred and twenty miles for a bag of imported coffee. I wanted to escape the ominous silence, as it demanded introspection, rectification, resolution and ultimate forgiveness.

On that day, life was simply too much. I needed to disarm myself, but the nearby Goldwater Air Force Range was testing bombs. The ground shook along with my nervous system. I remember feeling a high shrill crankiness and hearing an irritable voice in my head.

Later that day I was in a little shop that sold Mexican candles with various pictures of saints and the Lady of Guadalupe pasted on the glass holder. Accustomed to candle-lighting rituals, I purchased one and lit it on behalf of all the women like myself who aspired to a higher mood. Along with the Hatha-yoga, I also had mantras, prayers and Buddhist practices to see me through difficult times. Walking on the sun-parched terrain, I called on Tara, the Tibetan mother goddess of compassion: *Om Tara Tu Tara Tura Soha; Om Tara Tu Tara Tura Soha.*

The next day we met with new acquaintances who took us deeper into the desert. While driving out to an abandoned ranch, we debated the Tibetan concept of emptiness. The four of us began to explore, picking our way through cactus, washes and rock. We looked for rock paintings and scrambled up ledges to the surrounding caves. I looked at the clarity of the sky and recognized emptiness as the nature of my mind at that moment. When our guide returned with a javelina skull, cleansed by the desert's sun, I remembered, the proverb, "What's bred in the bone, is born in the flesh."

The day seemed unreal, with patches of color and landscape so strangely foreign it was similar to my internal vicissitude. The sun-bleached skull stripped away pretense. I thought to myself: here, conceptual reality meets emptiness more profoundly than anywhere I've ever been. I live in a realm of bone and breath—where flesh meets thought and objects come into existence—a realm where thoughts create form and bone becomes witness to our life.

HEADING EAST

We stayed in Ajo just long enough to have a desert adventure and gain a bit more confidence. Driving east, reality and metaphor mingled as we traveled on through the Texas Gulf Coast and along Louisiana and Mississippi's shoreline. We drove, pulling the antique Airstream out of Alabama across the Mobile Bridge and into Florida's Gulf Coast.

Pensacola was my secret destination because, before leaving Seattle, a highly respected astrologer made a chart of my astro cartography. This type of astrology locates you in time and space, revealing geographical ley-lines where you will supposedly flourish.

At that time, I had no idea that my metamorphosis would be so difficult.

"Metamorphosis is a biological process by which an animal physically develops after birth or hatching, involving a conspicuous and relatively abrupt change in the animal's body structure through cell growth and differentiation. Some insects, fishes, amphibians, crustaceans, Cnidarians, echinoderms and tunicates undergo metamorphosis, which is usually accompanied by a change of habitat or behavior. "—Wikipedia

I came across the country blindly on a mythical journey into the dark recesses of my yet-unrealized character. I knew surrender to life's lessons would also strip me of false pretenses. In 1999, I walked away from my marriage with enough money to fund a new life. Arriving in Pensacola, I was way behind the curve. Intoxicated by the sea breezes and the charm of the city's historic district, I thought the astrologer surely must be correct.

I wanted to get off the road and get closer to that which was still unrevealed. Leaping before carefully looking, I naively purchased an expensive, poorly built building on Zaragoza Street in the heart of Pensacola's historic district. The neighborhood's gingerbread facades implied fairy-tale lives but what lay behind the façades on Zaragoza Street was another story.

My new home had a commercial space on the main floor and I quickly turned it into a yoga studio. Roberto and I lived above the commercial space surrounded by old oak trees. We had a view of the bay and the bridge that crossed over to Gulf Breeze. I sold the Airstream to the first buyer with cash, knowing all too well that it would just rust and rot in Florida's salt air, and traded the monstrous Chevy Suburban for another economical Volkswagen bug.

Not long after I bought the Pensacola property, Bikram decided to take some of his teachers on a trip to India. There was no place on this earth I wanted to visit more than Bharat Mata—Mother India. It was before 9/11, and I still had ample funds; so I signed on. Roberto couldn't believe that anyone would travel that far—let alone go to India for only two weeks. I thought it would be an excellent opportunity to see a bit of the country that was my spiritual home, and I was ready for another adventure. I arrived in Mumbai a day before I met up with the group. That first day, I went via ferry to one of the islands close to Mumbai's center of commerce. I remember seeing the grand edifice of the Chhatrapati Shivaji Terminus, Mumbai's extravagant railway terminal which was built by the British. It was a far cry from the nearby huge heaps of rubbish that were home to some of Mumbai's most unfortunate citizens. From my hotel window I saw a beach with people tending small fires, and while I stared down into this new world. I also noticed a few skinny horses on a dirty grey beach that was quite unlike Pensacola's clean white quartz sand. I was thrilled to be in India.

My memory fails me concerning the exact times, and sequence of the trip, but the episode I must write about is so funny and so ironic, and it is so ridiculous that I still laugh at my fate. Very soon, after our group assembled, Bikram had us on a bus, and we were off to an exclusive community owned by his good friend who was a member of one of India's wealthiest families. The destination was a fabricated imitation of an American suburb. I couldn't believe it. There I was in the land of the Vedas—a country with the richest spiritual history—and I was sequestered in a private community with split-level American styled, middle-class homes. Ohhhh, I saw red! Amidst the homes, Mr. Roy, the developer, had just built Bikram a brand new large mirrored yoga studio. Part of our daily experience was to do class wherever we were, and somehow, Bikram managed to arrange space to practice a heated class everywhere we stayed. So there, in this ridiculous copycat environment, we practiced in a brand new studio that was still off-gassing from the synthetic carpet and glues that held the large mirrors on the wall. If that weren't bad enough we were to stay in this sheltered environment for five days; leaving precious little time for me to see any of the India I dreamed of. I couldn't believe it. For most of my life, I wanted to get out of the suburbs and there I was, stuck again, in the most unlikely place in all of India. This Indian version of success came complete with a golf course and a country club. Finally, we left, but not until being invited to an Indian wedding, which included the arrival of the groom on a white horse and a dinner and dance held in the country club's disco.

Our next stop was Agra. We stayed at another five-star resort. These posh quarters were again not the India I intended to see. Bikram arranged our meals. I avoided thin-skinned fruits and vegetables; I brushed my teeth with bottled water, and I managed to stay healthy while many of my friends went down with dysentery. One day at breakfast, I was chatting with a young woman about how we might escape the group and explore Agra on our own. Bikram came up to us and said commandingly, "I want to see the two of you on the bus!" He knew. So again I couldn't escape his itinerary that included a shopping trip to a rug bazaar where he behaved badly, having the owner throw down hordes of expensive carpets only to have all of us walk out of the shop an hour later without purchasing even one. Of course, while we were in Agra, we visited the Taj Mahal, and we practiced a bit of Hatha-yoga on one of the side porticos, until a guard asked us to leave. I did manage to sneak out alone a few times and shop in a fabric store where I had a few garments made and had a treasured experience with the culture and its people. One evening in the hotel's dining room, Bikram entertained Paramahansa Yogananda's nephew, Bishu Ghosh, the son of Bikram's own teacher. I

was quick to get a picture of the three of us.

All too soon, the trip came to its end. I flew from Delhi to Amsterdam and then on to Atlanta. On each leg of the journey, I saw my world grow smaller and got a bird's eye view of the southern culture that I began to abhor. I remember how after disembarking the plane in Atlanta and finding the boarding area for Pensacola, the quality of the people changed. With each step toward Pensacola, my world along with my hopes was shrinking. On the plane home, a man tried to "pick me up" asking me to meet him at his hotel. Seeing Pensacola from my new global perspective did nothing to enhance its flavor.

The Clinton years heralded a false prosperity from which I benefited. Stock prices soared. My divorce settlement was a portfolio of stocks and bonds. By many standards, I was wealthy. With no experience managing money, the investment company that held the portfolio devalued me and tried to misguide me for their own advantage. I had much to learn.

Amazingly, I had good instincts. As 1999 moved into 2000, I kept requesting the money managers at Prudential in Seattle to sell off inflated equities and mutual funds and increase the cash in the portfolio. I felt the winds of change but the brokers did not believe that I could see into the future.

They were overly confident; they believed themselves brilliant and believed that the inflated portfolios they held were a result of their management skills. They wouldn't listen to me. They continuously cajoled me and told me: "Donna, you have no experience. If there would be a decline, the market will  always come back. Don't worry, you're in good hands."

And there I was, in the Deep South the year George W. Bush was elected and 9/11 destroyed America's innocence. On that day, the markets crashed along with the planes that flew into the twin towers. What was I—an inexperienced, newly divorced suburban yogini from the liberal West—doing in a Republican, redneck, backwater, and military town? I had a huge mortgage, an enormous loss of portfolio value and an untrustworthy partner. Under the worst conditions and reasons, I had opened a yoga studio in a town that thought yoga was a by-product of yogurt, believed that Christ had died for everyone's sins and felt that the practice of yoga was blasphemous!

I had been told that for every year married, it takes a woman six months to get a foothold on her life. So, I had a twelve-and-a-half year learning curve ahead of me.

Over the course of three years I taught thousands of Hot Yoga classes to the brave souls who crossed my threshold. The high-priced building in Pensacola's historic district also made a bit of history. It was the first yoga studio on the Mississippi Gulf Coast, so I aptly named it Gulf Coast Yoga-A Bikram Method Studio.

By the time Christmas came around the first year, I was so tired that I was sure my death was near. I followed the training schedule with two classes each day and one on Saturday. No one who came had done the practice previously. Therefore, no one attending could model any of the asanas. I put volumes of energy into each person, hoping that they would return regularly, but there was a constant turnover of students. They came and went, some from the military stationed briefly in Pensacola and others who used the studio as a means to detox from weekend alcohol and substance binges.

But there was also a core group of truly good-hearted people who came regularly. They had faith in me when I had none in myself. It was just the beginning of my trial by fire.

Like an Indian marriage, again I had no choice. I learned to teach Hatha-yoga. I learned to recognize people's liabilities and frailties. I learned to show up when I didn't want to. I learned consistency and repetition. I learned that I was capable of working hard.

I also realized that in the back of our minds or one's developing perception, we come to know yoga as a metaphor for our lives and at some point our lives become the reflection of our yoga. That's when we begin a spiritual transformation. According to King Solomon, discipline is the beginning of wisdom.

TRIAL BY FIRE

COURAGE: synonyms—
Bravery, courageousness, pluck, pluckiness, valor,
fearlessness, intrepidity, nerve, daring, audacity, boldness,
grit, true grit, hardihood, heroism, gallantry; guts, spunk,
moxie, cojones, balls.

Bikram is a controversial Bengali man from Calcutta who lived in Beverly Hills. According to himself, he is a man with titanium cojones.

Soon after I opened Gulf Coast Yoga, Bikram called all affiliated studio owners to Los Angeles to discuss the franchise agreement he was conjuring up. It wasn't so much that he wanted to "own" yoga. He just wanted to protect the method, according to promises he made to his guru, Bishnu Ghosh.

He also wanted to protect us—his army of teachers who underwent the rigors of his training methods and the expense we incurred—by creating studios according to his standards. I have no doubt that Bikram wanted the best for us. I was happy to be back in Los Angeles with other enthusiastic studio owners.

When Bikram entered the room, it was clear that he had business on his mind. He immediately declared that, "No uncertified teachers will EVER teach in an affiliated Bikram studio." I made the mistake of teaching someone to lead my classes so that I could go to the meeting. I desperately wanted to belong to his extended yoga family and become a successful studio owner. Due to the economic tumble, I was concerned about closing my fledgling studio even briefly. With no other certified teachers around, I made the appalling and unjustifiable mistake of training someone to fill in for me.

There I was in the meeting, with maybe seventy-five or more other teachers and studio owners seated in a semi-circle around the boss. I said, "Bikram: I couldn't be here unless an uncertified person was in charge. I am a pioneer on the frontier."

You could feel the sway in the room as everyone's energy moved away from me. The overall feeling in the room was almost funny because it was so evident, palpable and visceral. For a short moment I was a pariah—an outcast and an untouchable.

Then, referring to me as Pensacola, the boss said, "I like you but if you don't listen to me, you will burn!" When he said, "I like you," the energy in the room swayed back toward me.

While we were all enjoying dinner that night in the lobby of the La Cienega Studio, Bikram's then new super-sized location, I received a phone call from Florida.

The young woman I trained and left in charge had an experience that would shake her and the neighborhood to their core. Unbeknownst to me, she had married a menacing, military maniac and was in a dangerous relationship. I didn't perceive Angela's desperation when she came to me asking to learn the practice.

While I was enjoying the ambiance of Bikram and Rajashree's catered dinner party, something unbelievable happened back on the Gulf. By the grace of God, after the evening class, Angela got into her car, turned the key and quickly realized that she had left the door to the studio unlocked. In a rush, she got out of the vehicle and went back to the door. Just when she was far enough away, an explosion rocked the entire historic district, shaking and shattering the otherwise sultry southern night.

The whole neighborhood reeled. Her husband had enabled an explosive device in her car. One of the old oak trees next to the building caught fire and my new Volkswagen bug melted. The house and the studio were singed and charred and the second-floor deck began to burn. Sirens from both the fire department and the police department stirred everyone's imagination. Flames shot so far upward they were seen all the way across the bay.

However, it was not the time for the young woman to depart this planet. Her forgetfulness saved her from an atrocious, deadly situation. I received a phone call from a good friend narrating the sequence of events. Standing in the midst of Bikram's dinner party, after hearing "the boss" say, "Pensacola… if you don't listen to me, you will burn!" left me in a state of astonishment. Believe what you will, but do believe me on this: I've seen things.

I've seen Bikram's yoga siddhis appear in small matters—seeming manifestations of psychic power. I've seen the clarity of his mind know things that might seem unknowable to the average person. I've seen him demonstrate asana and appear to be a genie coming out of a bottle, growing larger than life as he went deeper into the pose.

I am not saying that the boss caused the fire, but I am asking you: What do you believe? Was it coincidence or consequence or premonition?

PENSACOLA: IN AND OUT OF THE YOGA ROOM

Initially, I was so charmed by Pensacola's sea breezes and sugary-white sand beaches I didn't see the God-fearing racism and other forms of segregated ignorance disguised beneath the smarmy southern hospitality.

The Confederacy was alive and well on the Gulf Coast. Pensacola, just across the Mobile Bay Bridge, had roots deeply entangled with southern polemics. Having lived most of my adult life in Seattle, Washington, I had no experience with that kind of narrow-minded, God-fearing, two-faced bigotry.

After I returned from Los Angeles, matters got even worse. I noticed a noxious quality in the air that intensified my queasy feelings. Despite the sparkling emerald sea and the white quartz beaches, something was amiss.

Under the dazzling skies, Monsanto's nearby petrochemical company had contaminated the groundwater and the air. I saw toxic energy creating fuzzy, mirage-like distortions. Cancer rates were exceedingly high not only from six Superfund waste sites but also from toxins released from paper mills, power plants and discharges from the chemical companies.

In Pensacola, I was out of sync with sacred time. On Saturday night, street preachers shouted warnings of hell, fire and brimstone in front of the historic district's nightspots, frequented mostly by military personnel. I also could not comprehend the man who wore a loincloth and regularly hauled an enormous wooden cross on his back over the Bay Bridge. One of my students told me that I would never fit into the southern culture because I didn't know how to make small talk and throw compliments around like colorful wedding confetti when I met other women. Some came to my class expecting to find a bona-fide guru. I never failed to disappoint.

In search of companionship, Roberto and I found a small jewel on the Emerald Coast. Across the bridge in Gulf Breeze, in a cute office park/shopping mall, we discovered the practice room of a Tibetan sangha. Once through the doorway into the shrine room, my spirits soared when I saw the beautiful Thanka paintings and smelled the aroma of holy smoke.

We met Khenchen Tsewang Gyatso Rinpoche and his attending monks who, when visiting Florida's panhandle, blessed the sangha with Tibetan empowerment practices. Because we lived above the yoga studio in spacious quarters, we were quickly called on to occasionally host the visiting monks. Getting ready for Khenpo's visit, women came to the yoga center to help clean and prepare the meals. The place sparkled. Yet, while I enjoyed the process of readying for the honored guests, I knew down deep that this too was not it. Neti-neti.

DIVINE PROVIDENCE

Miracles are thought to be highly improbable events or luck but nothing is really random. There are causes and effects and there is a source of all things, both good and bad.

While living in Pensacola, not a day went by that I did not pray to get out from under the huge mortgage and the toxic atmosphere. Soon after purchasing the property, I put it back on the real estate-market. After being freed from an emotionally abusive marriage, it was incomprehensible to me that this Republican backwater, redneck, racist region would be my final destination.

The building had many structural and electrical problems while the yoga studio on the ground floor created problems of another sort. Our neighboring redneck lawyer enjoyed using his clout to bully us whenever he could. With a cigar dangling from his lips and a snide attitude, he threatened to close the access to the yoga studio. The walkway was on his easement. Every day began to feel like a bad movie. I couldn't believe the lessons I was meant to learn. Day by day, the promise of a brilliant, happy future seemed less likely.

All Roberto wanted was the easy life and a bit of notoriety. When our circumstances became complicated, we began to quarrel. I slowly came to realize that he was seeing another woman in Seattle and had expected me to subsidize his trips back to the West Coast on the plea of seeing his daughter.

Having had enough of his two-timing, self-aggrandizing usury, I told him we were over. He was close to sixty years old and penniless without me. Confronted with that reality, he ranted and raved and carried on something awful. He caterwauled like a cat whose nails were being torn off little by little. I carefully considered all the angles of our situation and decided to send him to Bikram's yoga training. The nine-week training was a big price for me to pay. Yet, I have always found generosity to be the right path. Part of the deal was that he would return to Pensacola and help me when I needed assistance.

Still estranged from my elderly parents due to Bob's scandal-mongering, I was drowning in sorrow and stress. One afternoon when I was sitting on the second-floor deck working on a stitching project, I received a surprising phone call from my mother, asking me to help her with my father. She confided that she wasn't feeling well and he was in a nursing home. By then Roberto had finished the yoga training and was celebrating his victories in Seattle. I had to plead with him to come back and live up to his end of the bargain. He did.

A dear friend of mom's met me at the Fort Lauderdale airport and filled me in on as much detail as she could. When I entered my father's room I saw a frail skeleton of an old man but his bright blue eyes revealed his passionate intensity. I immediately realized he was dying from congestive heart failure and I was shocked to discover that he was required to have physical therapy each day so that the nursing home could be remunerated for his care. Without delay, I arranged for his transfer to the nearest hospital hospice unit where he could die in peace.

On the only visit my mother was able to make to his bedside, the doctor pulled her aside and told her how valuable my advocacy had been. (My stock was beginning to rise.) I stayed by my dad's bedside, sleeping on a sofa in his room for two weeks. I phoned my mother daily to report on his condition. When Ben was in duress, I sang Jewish songs to him and, though my voice was weak and tentative and the words not clear, my attempts seemed to comfort him. Ben's last words were, "I am leaving now, and I will never forget you." After my father had passed away, I helped my mother with the funeral and stayed with her until she felt she could manage on her own.

Returning to Pensacola, I continued to teach classes and pray for respite from my difficult circumstances. My mother and I spoke on the phone regularly. Regardless of the huge mortgage and not fitting into the southern culture, the building's structural problems, a strenuous yoga schedule, a two-timing partner and low funds, I was happy because a miracle had occurred: my mother saw my person-hood for the first time. I was fifty-four years old.

THE DOLDRUMS

Back on the Gulf, I spent long weekends in the upstairs living room watching marathon episodes of The West Wing. Sometimes, to break the monotony, my genius friend Paul, with severe bipolar disorder, would take me cruising on his makeshift African Queen, a hand-built runabout. At home I painted and knitted and continued to teach the yoga classes, passing the time unsatisfied and fearful of wasting my life.

I was in the doldrums. Time dragged on until I received another phone call from South Florida. That same good friend of my mom's called me to Helen's bedside. Hospitalized with pancreatic cancer, she was in rough shape. This time Roberto responded quickly and I left everything in his care.

My little Chihuahua, Uma (whom I acquired shortly after settling in Pensacola), and I traveled south to stay with my mother for the painful duration of her life. Again, as with my father, I became my mother's advocate—she didn't want interventions. What she wanted was time for herself.

For more than fifty years she tended to my father, fixed his meals exactly as he demanded, lived in terror of his tirades and bad manners, and hid in her bed with her ladies' magazines and a small golden pillbox with bite-sized pieces of tranquilizers neatly arranged and close by.

When I brought her home from the hospital, I slept in her bed, right by her side. In the morning I made her vegetable juices that were easy to digest. She responded well to the change in diet and, for a while, thrived on the sattvic, gentle organics. But the diet couldn't save her. The cancer was too far spread. She soon declined but she never ever complained. Little Uma settled onto mother's bed and remained her constant companion throughout the ordeal.

The condominium development in its inception was primarily a Jewish enclave. My father chose it for the golf course and its country-club atmosphere. As time wore on, the area became popular with emigrating Haitians and other island peoples. Many of the emigrants worked in the medical system in all possible positions. We were fortunate to have certified nursing assistants close at hand. Though I was there for meals, support and decisions, I did not have to tend to my mother's hygienic needs.

The hospice workers and the Haitian women who lived nearby never let us down. Helen and I were both supported by a dedicated team of professionals who also became caring friends. When it looked as though death was imminent, the social worker on the hospice team recommended that I project my life into the future. I did so by enrolling in Gabriel Cousens' Mastery of Spiritual Nutrition program.

Shortly after my mother passed on, Hurricane Ivan, a deadly Category 4-5 storm, landed in Pensacola with frightening destructive force. I watched from afar on the weather channel as the storm rolled in and demolished beachfront property along Pensacola's delicate Gulf Coast. The violent winds sent debris crashing inland, leaving only scattered skeletons of homes along the delicate barrier island. Inland, roofs were torn off and boats landed upside-down in the city park. It was widespread chaos.

The yoga center's roof was partially destroyed, but the building—as poorly constructed as it was—remained intact. Finally, my property was at a premium because beach residents needed shelter inland while their beachfront homes were rebuilt. The building sold. I was redeemed. From those days forward, acts of God visibly began to loosen the chains that bound me.

UMA

BUILDING A LIFE

After packing my belongings in Pensacola, I went back to South Florida and remodeled mom's condo to suit my taste. I had black-and-white tiles put down, reminding me of a Parisian atelier. I had new carpet laid on a curve, giving the small space the illusion of size. I made the dining room into my painting studio, and created gallery space to display the paintings. Paul came for a lengthy visit to help me with the renovation. We designed built-in bookshelves that curved around the corners. We added an unlikely rough-hewn beam over the kitchen island, changing the staid environment into a truly cozy garret.

Though the apartment was comfortable and magazine-worthy after due time, I realized I couldn't live out the rest of my life in that condominium development. I still hadn't found my purposeful life.

For nine months the condo life was perfect while I wrote the papers and studied Gabriel's course material. I maintained my yoga practice in a close-by Bikram studio and shopped for my groceries at an organic farmer's market on Hollywood Beach. Yet, still I knew, this wasn't it. Neti-neti.

I also spent a bit of time investigating real estate. I visited many condo developments that were just breaking ground. It was right before the subprime mortgage fiasco when prices were ridiculous and most projects were sold out on speculation.

While I studied, I also associated with a unique Jewish community led by the young Rabbi Marc Labowitz. All the Labowitz family were Reconstructionist rabbis: mother, father and brother. Marc is a scholar and great teacher. I loved going to his Kabbalah classes. However, that too was not it. Neti-neti.

When the time came to attend Gabriel's thirty-day intensive program in Patagonia, Arizona, I knew I had to make a new life. I kept thinking I was getting older but the yoga practice kept me vital. I was not ready for the uninspiring retirement community. I realized that my life was before me not behind me. It was time for a new residence that would reflect my inner longings for peace and solitude, clean air and a lifestyle that would not depend on a car for daily necessities. I longed for a place where I could be free from gross materialism. After fifty-five years of responsibility to others, I was ready for something else.

PATAGONIA

After collecting my bags at the Tucson airport and with Uma safely in a carrying case, we made our way in a rental car toward the Tree of Life Rejuvenation Center. The drive from the airport to Patagonia is approximately sixty-five miles. Once off the freeway, without traffic signals or businesses along the route, I began to feel less manipulated and more alive. After driving over a small mountain pass, the Huachuca Mountains generously began to expand my vistas.

Arriving in Patagonia, en route to the Tree of Life, I passed a ramshackle property directly across from the post office. At first glance, the post office, with its American flag flying high over the walkway and a recycling center at the far side, appeared to be the headquarters of an outpost or camp.

Directly across the road I noticed two metal buildings surrounded by chain-link and tin fencing. I also noted substantial and neatly stacked rubbish and metal piles. The "For Sale" sign on the well-situated property immediately rang my bells, making me sit up and pay attention. I knew by my previous foray into real estate that this property had to be affordable because, other than its excellent location, there was nothing recommendable about it. I also knew that I had enough renovation experience to take it on.

I had one of those odd feelings when time seemingly stops and the spectrum of light narrows, propelling the present moment into the future.

2005

2016

TRANSFORMATION...
AN ASHRAM, A TEMPLE

The decision to buy the property was made the instant I saw the "For Sale" sign.

Everyone, including my realtor, tried to dissuade me from purchasing the old doublewide mobile home on a large, cluttered, dusty lot. The second metal building, only twelve feet wide by forty feet long was once the town's hardware and feed store and had been converted into a dreary but functional apartment. I was not put off by the amount of work the property needed and, since I had completed all the course work for Gabriel's program before arriving in Patagonia, the way was clear for me to negotiate the sale.

After the thirty-day program of live foods, a seven-day fast, afternoon and evening lectures, yoga and all the other activities I was keen on, Uma and I flew back to South Florida at month's end to close up the condominium. I finished the business of my mom's life and put my own life in order. That also took thirty days.

Once the car was packed and the moving van loaded, we again headed west. I was excited about life on the high-desert mesa and being part of what seemed a healthy community with a spiritual focus.

The first night in our new home we slept on a borrowed mattress on the floor of what was to become a den, which would eventually overlook a landscaped garden. But for the moment, it was a closed-up room surrounded by chain link and an eight-foot-tall tin fence running the entire length of the property. There were many nights when I pulled the covers over my head and heard mice scramble in the adjacent living room and kitchen. I told Uma to do something about those mice, but she just rolled her eyes and went back to sleep.

I was on my own again in a strange world. The primeval desert and its nocturnal creatures and night sounds, plus its wind, the intensity of the sun, and ranchers and Hispanic families all contributed to this strange new environment where I again knew very little. But this time, the spirit of the Wild West invigorated me and my enthusiasm for what would come remained high.

Step by step, little by little, I went along, trusting the process. Absorbed by the renovation, I had little time to feel anything other than motivated by the work ahead. It took weeks to get the scrap metal and other debris cleared away. Every Friday, the head of the Tree of Life's maintenance crew would come by and generously pick up the designated piles that had to go to the landfill. Eventually, a continuously shifting workforce showed up.

We got the interior underway with new doors and windows and I began to paint the walls and remove the plastic built-in cabinets. We worked on the interior from August to February of that year. When signs of spring appeared, it was time to think about creating a protected sanctuary where Uma could live out her life, safe from any of the desert's critters. Nocturnal javelina roam freely after dark and in the early morning they rummage for whatever they can find to eat. Coyotes are always nearby while rattlers bake in the intense desert sun on nearby trails and gravel roads. Occasionally, mountain lions have been seen close to town.

Faithful to the regional style, I designed curved stucco walls with strategically placed gateways to enclose what would soon be a small enclave. I bought the cinder block in nearby Nogales and hired a crew from across the border to build the walls. They spoke little English and I spoke no Spanish. Gesticulating, I was able to communicate the style I had in mind. Following the aesthetic of Hundertwasser, an Austrian artist who said that there are no straight lines in nature, I had them create curves and rounded edges whenever appropriate.

We built a mammoth retaining wall to keep the back hillside from eroding during the torrential monsoon seasons. The laborers thought I was loco because, at that time, the trailer and the metal building were not yet renovated. Thinking that I was spending mucho bucks on surrounding two unworthy buildings with expensively crafted walls, they remained perplexed until the walls were complete.

I had the buildings wrapped in styrofoam, held in place with chicken wire, then covered with plaster and finally sprayed with brown stucco, making the hacienda come alive. I placed a mission-style fountain exactly in the middle of the property and created a habitat for the birds that annually migrate through Patagonia.

I had a philosophy about the work being done. I accepted the skills of whoever showed up; always grateful, I never expected perfection. I was told that I followed the Santa Fe style: imperfect, flawed but happily shabby-chic.

The focus of my home and the yoga studio is the landscaped garden, where I have planted fruit trees and temple bamboo. They keep company with two huge old mesquites that lend a bit of history to this place. The old mesquites have deep roots, holding their massive trunks upright in the intense desert windstorms. They are the behemoth giants of the garden.

Coming from Florida and Seattle, where the habitats are naturally green, I made a green oasis, more from habit than intention. I didn't think of myself as an ecologist; nor did I realize I was at the forefront of the up-cycling movement. I was simply doing what made sense to me. I was not interested in bigger or better. I just wanted a place where I could live out my days away from the hurts and humiliations I had known and also have the consistency to dig deeply into the whys, the wherefores, my purpose, and my mission.

At first, I made an ashram. The word ashram (also ashrama) comes from the Sanskrit root shrama, which means, "making an effort toward liberation." And, indeed, liberation from materialism had been my constant pursuit. Here in Patagonia I was as far from corporate America as I could be while remaining in the United States. I did succeed in making a creative life. However, I continued to struggle; disappointments were many; and Nirvana was not up the road or around the corner.

NETI-NETI

Gabriel Cousens' Tree of Life Café and Temple are magnificently situated on a high-desert plateau. But, sitting outdoors at the café while enjoying the live-food cuisine and the pristine beauty were not enough to keep me satisfied. Something vital was still missing. I knew that defining myself as a live-food vegan was not it. Neti-neti.

Disappointed again, I had no choice other than to remain in Patagonia and begin to make sense of my life in a remote town far from diversion or distraction. I had to appraise what I had going for me and rely on my creativity while keeping my faith in the omens and predilections as I saw them. Once again I was alone.

Though I was more interested in my internal landscape, longing for the correct spiritual alignment, I still had to participate in life. Yet, social events held no appeal to me. The associations I had, though lovely and kind, did not fill the space inside me that needed to know something I could not yet name.

When I was participating in the Tree of Life programs and teaching a bit of yoga there, I met Emma, Gabriel Cousens' mother-in-law, who at that time was in her mid-eighties. She had a reputation for being clairvoyant and, with her uncanny ability to say "what came through," people flocked to see her. Then still a spry little woman, Emma was enormously popular and loved to socialize and participate in any event she could. I realized I could take her to the local events and be part of life with a purpose rather than selfish sensory gratification.

Apart from taking Emma out to community events, I put myself into a self-styled retreat. I stayed behind my walled garden for many years. I read and painted and studied, prayed and meditated.

EMMA

MIND OVER MATTER...
THE ARTS

A transcendentalist should always engage his/her body, mind and self in relationship with the Supreme; he/she should live alone in a secluded place and should always carefully control his/her mind. He/she should always be free from desires and feelings of possessiveness.
—Bhagavad-gita 6.10

Patagonia is an especially unique little town. Nestled between the Mexican border and the Patagonia Mountains, it remains true to its idiosyncratic nature. The air remains clean, with little traffic and no industrial pollution. We have neither global corporations nor banks. It is a place where one can empty one's mind of unnecessary clutter and live quietly in a small town where each day is usually the same as the previous one.

The populace of Patagonia is a mixed bag. Old hippies hold fast to old ideas. Retirees love hiking and bird-watching and mingle with ranchers and Mexican families who have widespread roots. Free from distraction and diversion, I have had the opportunity to focus my mind on the creative projects in front of me.

The yoga of living simply suits me. As I am writing this, I am listening to the wind in the mesquite trees surrounding my study, while thunder only a short distance away promises rain. The weather reminds me of life's miracles and the repetitive quality of each day makes the simple but important aspects of living satisfying. Centered in my kitchen, being one-hundred-percent responsible for my diet, I have been able to take care of my basic needs in an intelligent way and to develop life skills that have been essential for my good health, both mentally and physically. Though successful in these ways, I was still missing something I could not yet name.

ART AND YOGA *
MY FORTE

Often, my solitary time could feel more like a burden than a blessing. Yet, time without interruption did give me the opportunities I had always wanted to again pursue photography, painting and textiles. My creative work was always about process and understanding. Here again, I was not interested in entering the material world any further. I made art to have a dialogue with my soul, not to be a merchant. So, joining the Patagonia Business Association or the local women's art groups didn't suit me either.

During Seattle's technological boom, I learned how to blend painting and photography. When I decided to pick up a camera again, so many years later, my equipment and software were out of date. Deciding it was time to upgrade, I bought an iMac, a new pro-Canon camera and the latest software.

These investments took another significant learning curve. The long hours I spent sitting in front of my computer screen, though enthralled with the latest technology, were detrimental to my health. Since childhood, I struggled with a misshapen

sacroiliac joint that created a pelvic traffic jam. Sitting long hours made the condition worse until I could no longer ignore it.

Walking three steps was agonizing. I was gimpy and lame. While portraiture and painting absorbed me, gravity was not so kind. Facing decrepitude, I went back to what I knew—Bikram's hot yoga. I started to make the drive to Tucson three times per week to attend classes at Yoga Vida. I was so handicapped that I could not stand up straight when exiting the car or walk without debilitating pain in my left side. I went into the hot room and began the intense process of recovery. Everything hurt. I was ashamed of myself for the deterioration. In the studio, I was one of the remedial yogis. When class was finished, I went next door to the Whole Foods Market and pleaded for ice bags from the meat counter to pack over my hips for the drive home. Sitting after an intense practice was not the best option.

Sunday-morning classes were my favorite. The practice began at 8:00 a.m. I arose at 5:00 and began chanting various mantras, getting ready for the sunrise drive. I proceeded in silence and remained in silence until the class ended. Then, once again, I went next door to plead for my ice. I did that for some months and, within a reasonable time, I began to regain some flexibility and relief from the pain.

Transformation was occurring on a multitude of levels. I was considering making a guest house out of the second building which I had turned into a photography studio. Portraiture in Patagonia was limited. I did what I could and then it was time for another change.

Patagonia attracts tourists who enjoy birding and hiking. Yet, when I realized that inn-keeping meant housekeeping, I swiftly changed my mind. I was in a quandary when a friend came to me one day and said, "Doniji, what are you waiting for? Put a hot yoga studio in that building. I promise you they will come."

Reluctant at first, I thought that an older community in the desert would not support a successful studio. I had to reconsider the nature of success. It no longer felt right for me to make the long drive into Tucson so many times a week. I was getting tired of the impersonal teaching styles that were appropriate for an ever-changing clientele. It was time for me to step up and do what I was capable of and, when I did, the transformation of myself, the building and the nature of my life occurred at lightening speed.

Bart Young, a talented artist and builder, offered to design and construct a Santa Fe-style front for the metal building, which would blend beautifully with the existing renovations. He installed imposing posts set on rock pilings, along with a massive overhead beam, converting a once-inconsequential metal building into a charming studio. Like my home, we covered the metal siding with plaster and stucco.

It was early March of 2011 when I began teaching again. Nervous and not in the best of condition, I started and folks did show up. A core group of health-minded women joined me. When there was only one or two or three, we would practice together as we still do. I carried on by myself for quite a while. There was much to do in maintaining the property and teaching the classes. Although I had a strong facade internally, I felt my lack of partnership was indicative of a flaw in my character. I was envious of seemingly happy couples.

TOMMY AND THE RINPOCHE

One pivotal morning Tommy showed up in class. He owned property not far from me while maintaining another residence in Chicago. He came to Patagonia when he could in order to renovate his little guest-house. Coinciding with the opening of the yoga studio, Tommy began to spend more time in Patagonia. We became fast friends and then a couple.

Tommy doted on me and he helped me with everything. I believed in our future together. It seemed that our interests and our blended finances were beneficial for each of us. By combining our resources, we could also benefit the community by offering my yoga programs. We spent our first year together happily. Soon after he moved into the little yoga center, I went off on my second trip to India, which I had booked before our union.

Months before meeting Tommy, I traveled to Boulder, Colorado for an intensive teaching by Dzigar Kongtrul Rinpoche. For ten days, I commuted from Boulder to beautiful Ward, Colorado, where the estimable Rinpoche gave profound teachings from the three schools of Buddhism.

With the luxury of time, we went from the Theravada up through the Mahayana into the lofty heights of the Vrajayana. Not yet aware of the limitations of the Buddhist/impersonalist view, I was most impressed with Kongtrul Rinpoche's psychological savvy: "With the dharma, we can work with our life. We can work with what it brings us. We have the tools, the remedy, to work with our mind. The blessing of the dharma enables us to work with what life gives us."

Rinpoche went on to say, "Without self-reflection deep joy is not possible. When mind slows down it is in a deeper level of consciousness; transformation takes place." I loved all the pithy little sayings.

Buddhist ahbidharma, or psychology, was a fundamentally important rung on my yoga ladder. I loved hearing that wanting things to be different is a form of aggression. I found these statements irresistible: "You have to utilize the rough struggle." "Those who are awake live in a constant state of amazement" and "self-reflection is essential; the goal is to become softer and more open." "Have a deep yearning to learn and enhance your mind." "Don't make conclusions." "All the bad circumstances are what we practice with."

A few months later, Rinpoche's secretary sent out an email generously inviting his students to join him on his annual pilgrimage to Bodh Gaya. The price was reasonable and the thought of spending time with such an eminent scholar in India was too good to pass up. I imagined long, informative conversations and more profound insights. I quickly replied, "Thank you! I'd love to come along."

BUDDHIST INDIA

I wanted to gain experience traveling alone in India, so I chose to arrive a few days early and stay at a hotel separate from Rinpoche's entourage. Arrangements were made for me to be met at the airport by the owner of the guest house where I would be staying, both coming and going. When I left the gates and entered into the chaos outside the terminal doors, I found two men holding a placard with my name on it, and without doubt or worry I sped toward my awaiting adventure.

I arrived at my hotel just before sunrise and slept for a few hours. When I awoke and went to the window, I saw a narrow, crowded street with fruit and vegetable vendors on each street corner and a thick network of overhead wires.

Young college-age adults, on foot and on motorbikes with grimy, multi-colored faces, blasted paint guns at everyone and anyone. It was Holi, the advent of spring, when paint pigments are thrown into the air and at whoever is within reach. I grabbed my camera. A jubilant group of youngsters, with their arms opened wide and huge smiles, beckoned me to join them on the street. I thought this a wonderful welcome but I

declined the invitation. Staying in my hotel room, I watched safely from the window.

The following day I met up with Rinpoche's traveling companions at Connaught Place. Soon we would be together on an overnight train to Bodh Gaya, the home of the Mahabodhi temple and the Bodhi tree that marks the location of Gautama Buddha's enlightenment.

We spent the afternoon buying additional food for the train trip and other sundries we thought we might need. The following day, before boarding the train, we spent the day in the hotel lobby and restaurant, getting further acquainted with one another.

When it came time to leave the hotel and move toward the train station, Rinpoche's attendants hired porters to pull our luggage, stacked precariously on rickety handcarts, to the depot. When the train pulled into the Old Delhi Railway Station, it stopped just long enough for the suitcases to be deftly thrown onto the small boarding platform between train cars; the train would pull out of the station whether we were finished loading or not.

Once on the train, we were told to quickly find our sleeping quarters. My ticket brought me to a compartment with four Indian men. When they saw me, a Western woman, they looked on in disbelief. I also looked back in startled amazement. Pausing to gain composure, I quickly offered a quizzical smile, which also revealed my surprise, and in that way some of the tension was relieved. Then, none too soon, other women traveling with Rinpoche's group appeared in the aisle across from us.

I sat down next to a young man traveling to Calcutta, who was delighted to practice speaking English and asked me many questions about life in America. While we were conversing, I greedily stared out the window at the all-too-quickly passing countryside. I saw green fields, little mud huts, and conical-shaped structures that I thought were made of cow dung. This was a view of life I had longed to see.

The day soon turned to night. The chai wallah came through the compartments, followed by the dinner wallah, and then bedding was distributed to those who needed it. The train continued through villages and small towns until we all managed to sleep a bit before the 4:00 a.m. arrival in Gaya. We had to act swiftly again, as Rinpoche's experienced students offloaded the luggage. In the small morning hours, we made our way on a bus from Gaya to Bodh Gaya where we would stay at the Shechen Monastery.

We spent our week in Bodh Gaya making offerings of fruit bowls, prayers and flowers in and around the Mahabodhi temple. We also offered over seven thousand butter lamps over seven days. This trip was a Dana journey. Pronounced dah'na, it refers to giving and offering. We were with Rinpoche to support his generosity. At the Maitri Center in Bodh Gaya, we distributed fifteen hundred pounds of various grains to the low caste and outcaste. We also witnessed Rinpoche giving the founder and director of the Maitri Center an ample amount of money to support her endeavors for the coming year.

During the early evening, while sitting under the Bodhi tree, we listened attentively as Dzigar Kongtrul gave his dharma talks. When it was time to leave, we continued our pilgrimage to Varanasi via many of the notable Buddhist pilgrimage sites.

Our bus trip to Varanasi was exhausting as Kongtrul Rinpoche decided we would add other stops to our itinerary and make time-consuming detours. Not prepared for twenty-two hours en route, we had to put our best face forward. We left at 4:00 a.m. and arrived on the Ganges in Varanasi at two o'clock the next morning. During the night passage, a member of our group developed a horrible case of dysentery. The bus had to stop in remote and, I am sure in her mind, very frightening places. She and the women attending to her disembarked from the bus and disappeared behind bushes in unfamiliar terrain on a dark, moonless night. They created privacy for our ailing companion by screening her with shawls while she was plagued with all the horrors of dysentery. We who remained on the bus could feel her agony and her humiliation in the makeshift, countryside latrine. That experience had to be one of the worst times in her life.

When she and I first met at Connaught Place in New Delhi before our pilgrimage began, I noticed that she was agitated. From the very beginning, the whole scene overwhelmed her. I tried to comfort her but she scoffed at me. She seemed to resent my cheerful confidence. Nevertheless, I remained caring and came to her rescue by driving her across town with my hired driver when she became almost faint from worry and exhaustion. I was surprised when she got out of the car and, instead of expressing any gratitude, she offered me a condescending sneer.

She felt foreign to herself, and I was familiar with that state of mind from my previous trip to Thailand. Though I understood, I was also puzzled by how an older student of Rinpoche, a woman who had practiced for so many years, could be so rude with such little control or awareness.

While in Bodh Gaya at the Shechen Monastery, her fear and self-loathing continued to grow. She and I were chosen by the organizer of our pilgrimage to work together within a larger group, making flower offerings for the many altars and niches surrounding the temple. I became her projected target, as her not-so-subtle aggression was aimed at me. She tried very hard to make me the cause of her unhappiness/dis-ease. I continued to observe her discomfort, be impartial, remain neutral, and be happy regardless, which is fundamental Buddhist training.

A Buddhist teaching from the Four Immeasurables is to have "sympathetic joy for everyone." It is just good common sense to stay open, cheerful and confidant. When a "bad" thing happens, if we have enough practice—be it devotion, faith, meditation, or any of the yogas—we can begin to move from suffering to compassion to understanding. Thus, we can turn any circumstance into one that purifies. That's the way of the Bodhisattva.

I was with a group of people who had been within the most advanced Buddhist communities for many years. Many of Rinpoche's senior students, well into their upper sixties and seventies were original students of Chogyam Trungpa Rinpoche. I listened to many of them share high teachings and watched many of them behave without realization of these teachings. I witnessed little actualization. I was looking for the real deal! I wanted to be part of a community that had fundamental levels of actualized practice.

When we arrived in Varanasi, my suffering nemesis continued to feel abysmal and stayed in her room for a few more days. I expected her recovery would be humbling and that she would no longer aim her poisoned arrows at me.

An important aspect of Buddhism is the development of virtuous qualities. I naturally assumed that when she re-entered the group, she would be more humbly pleasant from her awful experience and kind to those whom she offended. She was a student of Tibetan Buddhism for over thirty years and, naively, I expected her to embrace the Four Immeasurables: loving kindness, sympathetic joy, generosity and compassion.

Is it because Buddhists, per say, do not believe in God that the teachings are often not sufficient to purify their character? I'm just asking. I know that the medicine for any illness is humility. I know that without obstacles, we may never rise above our current understanding. I know that without sadness, we may never develop empathy. Adverse events are situations that can benefit us when we counter those hard times with humility.

I was astonished when my traveling companion reemerged just as snappy toward me as ever. Her overall experience on the trip was sad to see. She had an excellent opportunity for transformation but somehow she did not have the awareness or courage she needed to recognize this episode as the great transformer it could have been. On that India trip, I frequently saw how knowledge without devotion and how intellects without devotion are breeding grounds for hypocrisy and self-centered arrogance. Humility is the essence of genuine spirituality.

> "A tree full of ripened fruit bows down naturally, because of the weight of the fruit and its willingness to make its fruit accessible to others."
>
> Swami Sivananda goes on to say:
>
> "Maya is so powerful that she deludes you every moment. Every moment she makes you feel that there is pleasure only in the sense-objects and nowhere else. You mistake pain for pleasure. This is the work of Maya. Beware. Remember Janma-mrityu-jara-vyadhi-dukkha-dosha,—this world is full of the pains of birth, death, old age, disease, and misery. There is no pleasure in these finite objects. Yo Vai Bhuma Tat Sukham. You can have Bliss in the Infinite alone. Sankirtan will enable you to realize this Infinite here and now. Sankirtan will save you from Maya, from delusion. Therefore sing the Names of the Lord always."

I observed numerous other behavioral discrepancies on that trip. I had intended to join the sangha, not to say that I was a member of an elite spiritual group, but to purify, educate, and actualize; therefore, I was observing with intention.

One day while still in Bodh Gaya we took a little trip to Vulture Peak where Gautama Buddha gave his most famous and defining sermon. We walked a long way on Bimbasara Road, the pathway the "noble ones" walked with the Buddha. Once we arrived at the top of Vulture Peak, with a view toward the Himalayan Mountains, my group began to chant the sutra: "The Heart of the Perfection of Understanding." The following is a short rendition of the HEART SUTRA.

BIMBISARA ROAD
THIS ROAD IS SAID TO HAVE BEEN
ORIGINALLY BUILT BY KING BIMBISĀRA WHEN HE
CAME TO MEET THE BUDDHA (C. 563–483 B.
C.) ON THE GRIDHRAKŪṬA HILL.

गर पथ
कहा जाता है कि इस ् क को प्राचीन काल में
राजा बिम्बिसार ने ्था जब वे गृध्कूट पर्वत पर
भगवान बुद्ध ८ ५६ ्३ ईसा पूर्व २ के दर्शन करने आए
थे।

Avalokiteshvara, the Bodhisattva of Compassion, saw clearly that the five aggregates of human existence are empty, and so released himself from suffering.

"Sariputra! Form is nothing more than emptiness; emptiness is nothing more than Form. Form is exactly emptiness, and emptiness is exactly Form. The other four aggregates of human existence—feeling, thought, will, and consciousness—are also nothing more than emptiness." "Sariputra! All things are empty: Nothing is born, nothing dies, nothing is pure, nothing is stained, nothing increases and nothing decreases. So, in emptiness, there is no form, no feeling, no thought, no will, no consciousness. There are no eyes, no ears, no nose, no tongue, no body, no mind. There is no seeing, no hearing, no smelling, no tasting, no touching, no imagining. No plane of sight, no plane of thought. There is no ignorance and no end to ignorance. There is no old age and death, and no end to old age and death. There is no suffering, no cause of suffering, no end to suffering, no path to suffering. There is no attainment of wisdom, and no wisdom to attain." The Mantra is thus: *Gaté, gaté, paragaté, parasamgaté. Bodhi! Svaha!"*

While everyone chanted, I sat aside, by myself. At that time, I hadn't realized that, for reasons not yet clear, I could not chant that sutra.

Even though I found my Buddhist traveling companions lacking manners, friendliness and actualization of their realizations, I was having a great time. My associations and conversations with Mother India's denizens were continuously interesting and expansive. I found the young and old filled with curiosity and a persistent desire to better their situations with an educational opportunity of any sort, which included speaking English with me. For instance, after we visited Vulture Peak, we went on to the extant remains of Nalanda University. Founded in the fifth century A.D., Nalanda was an ancient seat of learning. Over two thousand teachers and ten thousand students from all over the Buddhist world studied and taught at Nalanda. It was the first residential international university in the world. A walk through the ruins of the university takes you to an era when India imparted knowledge to the world.

Exhausted from the Vulture Peak expedition, instead of exploring the ruins, I chose to sit on a bench in one of the garden areas. While sitting, I noticed an Indian family, way across a lengthy field, walking directly toward me. When they arrived at my quiet place, they respectfully asked to visit with me. Of course I said yes and immediately they inquired if I was traveling with the Yogoda Satsang Society. I was surprised by the question. I acknowledged my past association with the Yogoda Satsang Society (which is Paramahamsa Yogananda's organization in India) but also told them about the nature of my current trip. Perhaps many Western tourists are associated with Yogananda's society, but then, sitting in the gardens at Nalanda University with my Buddhist traveling companions, it seemed quite extraordinary to me.

In hindsight, I realize that many Westerners begin their love affair with India by reading Paramahansa Yogananda's *Autobiography of a Yogi*. Also, many Westerners traveling in India are spiritual seekers of one sort or another. I was in a relationship with India's transcendent nature and I was gloriously happy.

My next encounter with Yogananda's lineage was in Varanasi. Followers of Samkhya philosophy consider Varanasi to be India's holiest city. On the shore of the great Ganges River a ritual fire has continuously burned for over three thousand years. You can expect to see all manner of people strolling along the river's edge alongside the ghats. Throughout Varanasi's back alleyways, handlooms continuously weave wedding fabrics and silks. Varanasi is home to Hindus and Muslims who live side-by-side sharing the tourist trade. It's common to see wandering sadhus pilgrimaging through the old city. The broad walk hosts morning and evening pujas and yajnas that are extraordinary: bells ring, enormous incense fires burn, speakers blast bhajans, fire torches deftly thrown continuously raise us up and wake us up, while tour guides as well as charlatans congregate for favors.

Mary, our tour organizer, told me not to speak to anyone as I strolled the ancient pathways. She said, "Donna, they know what you want to hear. They have been doing this for centuries. It's in their DNA. You are no match for the experienced one, whose whole family is dependent on you to earn a small wage." She went on to say, "Furthermore, they know what you want to hear and will convincingly tell you so. A Western woman dressed with an Eastern flair, walking alone on the ghat, is an easy mark."

We come to Varanasi as tourists, seekers, and aspirants. The reasons for visiting the old city, nestled on the banks of the Ganges are plainly visible on our faces and can be deciphered by our attire and demeanor. We might be a mystery to ourselves, but we are no mystery to those who need to earn their livelihood from our mystical musings.

On our first early-morning outing, we were told to pair up for safety. Some decided to see the puja from the river. A woman approached me to walk with her. Almost immediately after setting out, she left me standing alone on the walkway when she spotted a few of her friends farther ahead, who were renting a boat for the morning rituals. Pondering my situation, and recalling Mary's words, I considered returning to the ashram. Seemingly out of nowhere, a handsome young man appeared; he began to tell me just what I loved hearing. He fulfilled Mary's admonitions. He said, "Madam; I can tell you are a very spiritual woman; there's something special about you. If there is a way that I can help you, let me know. I will be your guide and take care of all your needs." I laughed and flattered him right back. Happily, I responded, "You are an adorable young man and I have been told to avoid handsome young men who flatter me with such praises. Therefore, I am going into this shop. Thank you very much; I wish you success." Ducking into the store, I was temporarily out of harm's way, with enough time to consider my situation. I spent some time looking at all the regional paraphernalia, and when I returned to the sidewalk he was still there with his ready, charming smile. The ashram at Assi ghat was nearby, and I said, "You may follow me to my lodging, and I will discuss your offer with my boss. Mary was just within reach when I recounted the events, saying, "Everything you said would happen did happen to me within ten minutes. However, I feel there is something special about this young man, and he wishes to be our guide." I knew Mary needed help in locating the temple she intended to visit. Trusting my judgment, she went out the gate and met Sunil. As he also charmed her, we struck a deal and soon were off to find the temple dedicated to the goddess Sati.

Sati was the daughter of Prajapati Daksha. Against her father's wishes, Sati married the god Shiva. Shiva and Sati were a couple of happy demigods when Daksha organized a great yajna. A yajna is an offering to the gods based on rites prescribed in the earliest scriptures of ancient India. A yajna is always purposeful, even though the aim may be as general as sustaining the natural order of the universe. Correct performance of the ritual and recitation of the necessary mantras, or sacred formulas, is considered essential, and everything must be in a high state of purity.

When Daksha organized his great yajna, he did not invite Sati or her husband, Shiva. Daksha did not want his daughter to have anything to do with the Lord of Kailash, let alone have her marry him. Against Shiva's wishes, Sati went to the yajna, where all the great demigods settled in among themselves. When Sati arrived at the ritual site, Daksha ignored Sati and vilified Shiva. Unable to withstand this insult, Sati jumped into the sacrificial fire and committed suicide. Sati died, but her corpse did not burn. Shiva went into a great rage and slew Sati's father, Daksha. The wild, grief-stricken Shiva wandered the universe with Sati's corpse. Finally, Vishnu dismembered the body of Sati into fifty-two parts, each of which became a Shakti Pitha, a temple of the goddess. Sati's earring is believed to have fallen at Varanasi, establishing Vishalakshi as a Shakti Pitha. Now, thousands of years later in this Age of Kali, women come to the temple and offer their jewelry on the steps to the well for a favor.

Mary wished to visit this temple and needed Sunil to lead the way through the twisting back alleys and walkways that threaded through the ancient city. Arriving there, we placed our shoes in the proper receptacle and purchased the necessary oblations to the Brahman priest situated on a podium near the entrance. We rang the brass temple bell to let the demigods know that we were there to make the appropriate offerings. Mary wished to make a prayer. The Vishalakshi Temple was one of the few near the Ganges that had a deep well filled with water from the holy river. I sat above Mary as she made her way down to the well, accompanied by one of the temple's Brahman priests.

Sitting above the well by the side of the steep steps, I began to ponder gods and goddesses, demigods, and Vedic history. I thought about my Jewish background. I thought about Old Testament Abraham, who abolished "idol" worship. I thought

about the place of Judaism in the history of religious development. Living as we are, in the Kali Yuga, the age of degeneration, I reminisced about the time I studied women's spiritual histories and about the coming of the patriarchs more than five thousand years ago. Watching Mary make her oblations, I sat, observed, and considered all that I had learned thus far about the history of religions, gods, and goddesses. Following Rinpoche's teaching—just stay open, I enjoyed the breath of creation while amazed that I was in this exotic place on this pilgrimage.

Sunil would not accept money from us for his services. What he did request from us was a visit to his "uncle's" silk showroom. He came from a family of weavers. It is more common to find Muslim families in Varanasi in the fabric business, but Sunil and his family were Hindu. Mary and I agreed to his conditions. It was an easy, delightful agreement for me. As a weaver myself, I felt weaving and making fabric to be a holy endeavor. It is painstaking slow. Threading a loom requires exacting mindfulness, making it a meditation and a labor of love. All through the back alleyways of the old city, handlooms beat the rhythm of the ancient culture into the cloth.

In the ashram on Assi Ghat, I shared a room with two young women who were horrified by the prospect of going into one of the fabric showrooms. One said to me, "Oh, Donna, be careful. They take you into a room filled with bolts and stacks of fabric. Then, a few men will begin to throw them all out on the floor." I eagerly looked forward to the experience. With no scare, fear or panic, my relationship with Sunil was on steady ground. Meeting his "uncle," seeing their showroom and spending a few dollars on shawls and scarves was my pleasure. When the time came to honor our promise, only one other woman would go. It so happened that when we arrived, the elder uncle was ill. The receptionist begged forgiveness and we were assigned a younger "brother." As I look back on these incidents, I realize how suave and savvy the sales approach was but, even so, I remained delighted by the events and their nature. A robust man in his mid-fifties entered the room. Once cold drinks served, the salesman began to tell us his story of how he recently became a member of the Yagoda Satsang Society. Was my association with Paramahansa Yogananda written on my face? There are many saints, sages and lineages represented in Varanasi. Was it coincidence, providence or clever sales? Could it have been a combination of all? I never mentioned anything about my history to Sunil but, just as Mary had said, he knew these things about me. He offered to make arrangements for me to visit the Lahiri Mahasaya temple and pass by the home of the famous sage and guru. While the fabrics were reeled out onto the floor, he continued stories about other tourists' pilgrimages to Varanasi and their various mystical experiences. He insisted on taking me to the Lahiri Mahasaya temple the next day but, due to our scheduled departure, there was no way I would leave the group for fear of missing the train back to Delhi. With parcels in hand, I thanked them kindly for the experience and with my beautiful new silks we returned to the ashram.

Early the following day we went on a final walking tour of the old city. Mary, who arranged the tour, shared with the hired guide how I had met so many people along the way who had recognized me as one of Yogananda's flock. Even though I was long passed my infatuation with Yogananda, I remained respectful. My connections to him began as a teenager and continued through my association with Bikram. Bishnu Ghosh, Bikram's guru, was the Paramahamsa's youngest brother. On my first trip to India with "the boss," I met and visited with Bishnu Ghosh's youngest son, Bishu, Yogananda's nephew.

Mr. Tawari, our walking guide, also declared, "I just joined the Yogoda Satsang Society." I am not a cynical person and all of these associations delighted me. Whether I was cajoled or not, I chose to believe in synchronicity and the law of attraction.

Lahiri Mahasaya was a direct disciple of the elusive wandering sadhu Babaji. Speculatively, Babaji was born Nagarajan and was considered to be Lord Shiva in his human form. From his guru Babaji, Lahari Mahasaya learned the ancient science of Kriya-yoga. When I came to India with Dzigar Kongtrul's extended sangha, I didn't have Yogananda or Bikram or Hatha-yoga on my mind, but India with her motherly transcendence kept showing me my roots and expanding my horizons.

Mr. Tawari told me I was blessed to have such associations in my life but the Lahiri Mahasaya temple was not on our tour. However, at the end of our time together, because it was not so far out of the way, he changed his initial plan and took us into the Mahasaya temple. The décor of the temple was different from the few Hindu temples I visited. Thinking

back to the Vishalakshi temple, with its constant clanging bells, priests to appease, oblations to purchase, and offerings to make, the Mahasaya temple was spacious, uncluttered and quiet. Mother India enthralled me with her esoteric secrets. She revealed histories and lineages that were important aspects of my spiritual quest. The threads of my life were becoming a colorful tapestry. It was evident to me that Yogananda's lineage came from the Himalayan Mountains and their practices were closely related to Buddhist teachings.

When I arrived home, I thought it would be a good idea to backtrack and take the Kriya-yoga initiation that was conveniently offered in Phoenix shortly after I returned. However, after practicing the spiritual science of Kriya, although I found it effective and engaging, I knew it would not offer me what I ultimately wanted. As yet, I did not know what that would be. There was always a nameless quality missing in each spiritual directive and each spiritual practice I attempted. Neti-neti. Again, I faced the shortcomings of each spiritual road I took. From Buddhism, I had the ability to stay with whatever arose and, even more challenging, to stay with whatever didn't arise. From Hatha-yoga, I was strong and engaged, healthy and alert but still, despite my accomplishments, something was missing.

KRISHNA CALLING

*"You own everything that happened to you. Tell your stories.
If people wanted you to write warmly about them, they
should've behaved better."*
—Anne Lamott

*SCORPIO (October 23-November 21): "There's a way not
to be broken that takes brokenness to find it," writes Naomi
Shihab Nye in her poem "Cinco de Mayo." I suspect this
describes your situation right now. The bad news is that you
are feeling a bit broken. The good news is that this is a special
kind of brokenness—a brokenness that contains a valuable
secret you have never been ready to learn before now."*
—Bob Brezsny, Free Will Astrology

*"When a pious person is in an adverse situation he turns his
attention to God. Thus, the calamities in life, which act as an
impetus for spiritual progress, are appropriately called yoga."*
—A.C. Bhaktivedanta Swami

It's odd how a life can change in the flick of an ash or blink of an eye or how a day may start with optimism and end with catastrophe. It's odd how a full moon lunar eclipse can influence the fate of the world and how disaster can strike suddenly— seemingly randomly—but not. We might think we can get away with murder or lie or cheat or steal, but it catches up with us.

A blood red moon is inauspicious. Eclipses herald new beginnings and frequently eclipses portend traumatic endings. I saw the eclipsed red moon as she sank below the horizon. I knew things were about to change. I chewed my lip and tore at my cuticles. I also sank low into what I recognized early on as a potentially menacing moment. I kept hearing the old Stephen Foster song, "Hard Times Come Again No More."

I am on intimate terms with my muse; she talks to me through music, painting and poetry. I recognize her signs and omens. I have faith and I knew I would need every bit of spiritual awareness, practice and purpose I had thus far developed to get through that time. She told me, right out, keep the right company or keep no company at all. My focus had to narrow. I had to sit and listen to the quiet. I had to get low and sink into the shocking after-effects of the assault. She told me to practice yoga for my sanity and that Krishna had arranged for me to have everything I needed. She told me to replace intoxication with sadhana. She, my ever-present muse, told me to get high with God and bow before the morning sun. She told me to know humility in all things. She told me to live apart but remain generous and then she told me to always tell the truth. She whispered even more quietly, "Donna, study the *Bhagavad-gita*."

"Humility; pridelessness; nonviolence; tolerance; simplicity; approaching a bona fide spiritual master; cleanliness; steadiness; self-control; renunciation of the objects of sense gratification; absence of false ego; the perception of the evil of birth, death, old age and disease; detachment; freedom from entanglement with children, wife, home and the rest; even-mindedness amid pleasant and unpleasant events; constant and unalloyed devotion to Me; aspiring to live in a solitary place; detachment from the general mass of people; accepting the importance of self-realization; and philosophical search for the Absolute Truth—all these I declare to be knowledge, and besides this whatever there may be ignorance." Bhagavad-gita As It Is 13.8-12

My day begins early. The ninety minutes before sunrise is the most potent time of the day for sadhana and prayer. I teach a 7:00 a.m. yoga class and the yoga room is across the yard. One glorious spring morning as I walked through my garden toward the etched glass lotus-blossom door, I noticed the Mexican primroses reaching upward toward the morning light. The lesson not wasted on me was the metaphor I needed for the early class. That morning my mind had been brought low, drawn down by what lay just below the surface of my consciousness. I knew the astrology was difficult and that my circumstances were changing. What was good began to sour. I was being cleansed. Krishna was calling. I felt the pull. Krishna's regulative principles are simple: no illicit sex; no intoxication; no gambling; no meat eating. Tommy and I were at odds. At that time he was a stoned, meat-eating, gun-carrying lunatic. I told him that coffee and pot would bring him down in the yoga room and it would only be a matter of time.

Sitting under my figurative Bodhi Tree, I knew something powerful was underway. I was walking the line between materialism and spiritualism. After years of analytical evaluations, neti-neti, something powerful was evidently influencing me. By afternoon the morning's angst softened. I sensed what was to come and I knew it wouldn't be easy or pretty. I was aghast watching Tommy lose his grip and descend further into darkness. I continued to witness his behavior become more and more aggressive but I remained stalwart. I knew there could be no possibility other than my redemption. I broke free from the past and now I had to end more associations. When Krishna is the future, why wallow? But like Arjuna, I had to be ready to fight. The muse checked in to see if I was prepared to lay the past aside and begin earnestly and I was.

Maintaining a steady stream of consciousness but not yet in Krishna's transcendental world, I moved through this sticky quagmire with Buddhist teachings. I had faith in the higher power that pulled me along. I received little nudges, stars winked at me, double rainbows appeared and encouraging paragraphs fell out of cyberspace. I saw omens in the difficult constellations. Krishna wanted me. My radar was working, my antennae upright. I had faith in something I still couldn't name.

There is a price for everything. Sometimes I felt like the grim reaper waiting for the axe to fall. Tommy frightened me with his rages. His eyes, razor slits like the devil's eyes in Rosemary's Baby, were in my face, telling me my life was about to change for the worse. I saw myself exiled from all I'd worked for; he thought he could take possession of my walled garden sanctuary. The night of his final assault, I told Uma and my new puppy Fu, that it is time to mourn. Tommy's got to go and not come back; we should wear armbands, cover the mirrors. (That's the Jewish tradition of mourning.) Drugs and dependency got the best of him. I thought I might do a fire ceremony and imagine myself on the banks of the Ganges, burning our remains on the ghat.

HARE KRISHNA

Mantras are the utterance of sacred sounds representing that which is beyond the material world.

Lord Shri Krishna in the Bhagavad-gita *(10:35.) says: "Amongst the chanted mantras, I am the Gayatri." OM bhuur bhuvah svah tat savitur varenyam bhargo devasya dhiimahi dhiyo yo nah prachodayaate—OM. I adore the Divine who illuminates the three worlds—physical, astral, and causal; I offer my prayers to that Supreme God, who shines like the Sun. May he enlighten our intellect.*

Repeating Gayatri each morning reminds us that we do not hold up the sun or create its heat. We are not the Supreme who keeps the constellations in the sky. Gayatri says: "I meditate on the sun god who is maintaining the three worlds." The Vedic name of the sun god is Savitur. The greatest Savitur is Krishna. Therefore, both mantras are meditations on Krishna, and Lord Shri Krishna is the supreme creator of everything manifest.

Additionally from the *Brahma Samhita* (5.27–28) it is stated: *"Then Gayatri, mother of the Vedas, having been manifested by the divine sound of Shri Krishna's flute, entered the lotus mouth of Brahma, the self-born, through his eight earholes. Thus, the lotus-born Brahma received the Gayatri mantra, which had sprung from the song of Shri Krishna's flute. In this way, he attained twice-born status, having been initiated by the supreme, primal preceptor, Godhead Himself.*

Enlightened by the recollection of that Gayatri, which embodies the three Vedas, Brahma became acquainted with the expanse of the ocean of truth. Then he worshiped Shri Krishna, the essence of all the Vedas, with a hymn."

The summer before Tommy went mad, when things at home were harmonious, I began to chant a version of the Gayatri mantra. I don't remember how I came to it, but I do remember that upon hearing it, I recognized its potency. Consequently, I was determined not only to learn it, but also chant to it one hundred and eight times at the appointed hours. Tommy had outdoor speakers wired in the garden. As I pulled weeds and watered, I chanted along with the recorded bhajan. Krishna was calling.

Looking back, all the circumstances that led me to Krishna Consciousness make sense. There was a definite chain of events leading me to understand Krishna's mercy, but then I was just following my numinous illuminations. Delving further, I wanted to see Krishna. I found the magnificent work of B.G. Sharma and I studied his gorgeous paintings. One of my yoga students, Eileen Losch, gave me Steven J. Rosen's book, *Holy Cow.* Krishna was appearing everywhere. Like Hansel and Gretel, I followed crumbs along the path. I didn't know where they led but, unlike the two folk children, I was being taken to higher ground.

As for Tommy, he continued to spiral down. He increased his meat consumption along with other intoxicants. The divide was growing and his mania was becoming blatant. I was in denial that our relationship was ending because I honestly believed our partnership was beneficial for both the community and us, and I believed he would right himself.

No matter what occurred, I had to show up in the yoga room. I had an obligation. Still chanting Gayatri, I began to think about how Bikram's method of yoga had been my bedrock for many years. I thought about how the practice had seen me through my epic divorce and the end-of-life care I gave my mother and father. I thought about how the practice kept me in good health. I knew I would be all right. I had faith and Krishna began to intervene.

One morning I awoke saying, "It's all for the love of Krishna." This surprising, out-of-the-blue statement kept drifting across my mind, like email notifications drift across my computer screen. From that day onward, everything I saw, every situation, every relationship, every hard time and every good time, was for the love of Krishna. Following the signs, I obtained a copy of Srila Prabhupada's Bhagavad-gita As It Is. Enthralled with its opening, I enjoyed reading his introduction and his analogy of how we must weed out what doesn't support our spiritual endeavors. We don't need to waste our time with hopeless people and impossible situations. "As in the paddy fields, the unnecessary plants are taken out."

EVERYTHING IS KRISHNA'S MERCY

Time went by and, alone again, I fell into a crevasse of quiet despair and ugly self-pity. I prayed to any god anywhere to vanquish my enemies. I was petulant, hurt, belligerent, foreign to myself and I knew better. Caught in reaction with tons of guilt and shame, my once-bright future looked bleak. I thought about Buddhist prayers and the Lord's Prayer. "Forgive me my trespasses as I forgive those who trespass against me." And she, my guiding voice, said, "Donna it's okay you have been vanquished for Krishna's benefit, you are angry, but this will pass." She told me to bow low and wait for the intercession and, she went on to say, "You are being cleansed of one hundred past-life sins, obscurations and obligations chant Hare Krishna."

Realizing that Tommy was a projection of my own desires, a psychopathic phantom lover, I had to ask myself, whom did I love? What did I lose? He sent me an email asking for money that he said I owed him. He asked me to bankroll his new relationship. My jaw dropped. The reminder of his sickness made me nervous. In another disturbing email that he sent after my beloved Uma passed on, he wrote, "You are all greed and ugliness." In the last line of the last email, he wrote, "I mean you no harm."

And yet, despite his spewed hatred and my knowing how mad he was, I still grieved the loss. I missed the person he promised to be. I loved him and as I watched him fall from the top of the mountain, I could do nothing to soften his landing. There was no chance of mediating this scenario. I loved a phantom made entirely from my projection. I had a front-row seat to a documentary film entitled: My Own Brand of Narcissism.

I asked myself, if love is not for THE LOVE OF KRISHNA, in service and devotion, is it true love or something other that we mistakenly cling to? I had to find the answers.

With my head in my hands, I sat upon the doorstep, ruminating on the nature of love. I had to look at my false assumptions. According to the Buddhist practices that I had been keen on, I was in Nirvana, embracing emptiness, impersonalism, and nothingness. Feeling the sadness and loss of my relationship with him, I had to admit to myself that I was in nowhere-ville. With a broken heart and a sense of overwhelming dismay, I had to ask myself, how did I fall into this dejected place and why weren't the many years of Buddhist practice helping me to abate this dismal, all-pervading misery? I needed answers. I needed help. With chagrin, humility, and dismay, I realized that I had outgrown Buddhism's nihilistic view.

Srila Prabhupada's purport, Chapter 6, text 38, in the *Bhagavad-gita As It Is,* reveals the state I was in:

"There are two ways to progress. Those who are materialists have no interest in transcendence; therefore, they are more interested in material advancement by economic development or in promotion to the higher planets by appropriate work. When one takes to the path of transcendence, one has to cease all material activities and sacrifice all forms of so-called material happiness. If the aspiring transcendentalist fails, then he(she) apparently loses both ways; in other words, he(she) can enjoy neither material happiness nor spiritual success. he(she) has no position; he(she) is like a riven cloud. A cloud in the sky sometimes deviates from a small cloud and joins a big one. But if it cannot join a big one, then it is blown away by the wind and becomes a nonentity in the vast sky."

Though philosophically wise, I was not happy. And I knew that the kind of happiness I sought rested on something other than temporal relationships or material gain or transcending the experience and taking comfort in its inherent nothingness. I needed to resurrect myself in a whole and holy new way. I needed to be resolute in analyzing my situation. The question that loomed the largest and most potent was, where does love go when a once-promising loving relationship breaks apart? Does the appreciation for a lovely rose vanish after it withers off the bush? I knew I was in a situation that would be a great source of knowledge—if I could discover the truth. Through dejection, pain, and suffering, distinctions and understandings that were foreign to my Buddhist mind were soon made known to me. Though coming to such heart-filled spiritual advancement via a road full of obstacles was hard, nevertheless, victory was on the horizon. The circumstances of my affairs were the conditions I needed. That's how Krishna's mercy works. He gives you what you need and you have to realize that what you see and how you are is a reflection of how you have been and what you have desired.

Accounting for my situation, I thought about my disciplines. I could sit cross-legged for hours at a time. I could recollect philosophies on the nature of mind. I could look outward at my accomplishments, and I could look inward with breath awareness. I could also pretend to be a victim of circumstance. But I knew better. I had already accepted that whatever happens in my life is my lesson plan. Therefore, the transitory, ephemeral nature of my life demanded scrupulous introspection, action and responsibility. Some things were just not lining up. When the foundation is not firm, eventually the building will topple. To build off of a mistake is another mistake. I knew I couldn't make a wrong thing better by adding distractions or being in denial or laying blame. I had to consider my rectification.

Krishna's mercy appears in many different ways. When one is able to see that difficult circumstances are merciful, the hard times are purposeful. Wisdom won from defeat on the material plane is victory. Krishna had my arms tied behind my back; I had to holler uncle and give up. "Thy will be done" in Sanskrit is referred to as Saranagati. It means to take shelter in the Lord. I realized there would be no other way for me, other than finding happiness in the Lord's shelter. When I realized that every act of creation is by the hand of God, whether apparently good or bad, I began the process of recuperation. Knowing I had gone astray, I proceeded to the yoga-room floor. Supplicating myself and humbly asking for help and guidance was the beginning of the most profound mercy my life has thus far received. I knew that the immediacy, humility and intensity of my prayers and supplications would reflect the depth of the answers I would receive. The hard times and challenging circumstance called for knee-bending humility. The knot I found myself in was tighter than my usual mystically-minded muddles. When one is tied up in knots, there is no room for divine intervention. Relaxation in the form of shradda, or faith in the process, and saranagati, surrender, is the sanctified place where change or mercy occurs.

The way our relationship ended, though not entirely abrupt, was traumatizing. It was emotionally violent. I hurt deeply and I was not only scarred but also scared.

Soon after our demise, Tommy flaunted another woman in my face. Dancing through our little town during the Fourth of July festival, he showed everyone how little I mattered to him. People came to me and reported, "Donna, I saw Tommy with his new girlfriend. She looks much younger than you." As if we were teenagers! Dignity went out the window with Tommy. (Humiliation and public shame were the ingredients I needed to go to the place where I had to beseech the Lord for help in understanding.) Now, I am grateful for the events that occurred, but then I was in shock.

Once again, facing life alone in a small town that held very little variety left me frightened. I hurt to the core. I couldn't imagine his making our commitment to one another so trite or so disposable. The aftermath of this experience left me bitter and my bitterness began to poison me. My soul had an infection. I had to find the remedy to this malady. Hatred, hurt, isolation and alienation were not acceptable responses. Those emotions are poison. Yes, of course, there is a period of grief when one loses a loved one. Grief is a high-minded emotion. Grief softens the heart and enlightens the soul. But what I was experiencing was different from that. I was dejected, dismayed and bitter. I had it upside-down and I needed to know how to turn myself right-side-up. In response to such intense, uncomfortable emotions, I closed down. I became misanthropic and avoided everyone.

Picture this: a small town, less than one thousand residents. There are two main thoroughfares with only a few side roads and alleys. I maintain a yoga center. Tommy keeps a guest house that I designed, decorated and refurbished. Both of our properties are highly visible from the main road. And, we both must pass each others residence in the course of daily life. As I would walk past his home, I would try very hard not to look. That didn't work. I felt trapped and cornered. His place, the Pink Adobe Guest House, was furnished and refurbished by me. Separating myself from these artistic expressions was the painful impetus I needed in order to understand. I had to ask myself, how do I walk past here each day and remain open?

I began to parse out my emotions as one would parse a sentence or a mathematical equation. What was I looking at? If it were just a painted building, why would it cause me such distress? Why was I torn between looking and turning away? When I looked, I was confused and when I turned away, I was blocked. I began to realize the answer lay in this conundrum.

DISCOVERY

Compassion is the core of all Buddhist practice. While parsing out my difficulties, I looked at all the elements that comprise goodness. I longed to feel good again. I wanted to be good again and stop waging an internal war against myself and everyone else. One morning, while I was thinking about love and my predicament, a friend dropped by. She only wanted to entertain herself briefly before going to lunch and questioned me about the nature of my mind. I replied that I was deciphering whether love and compassion are one and the same. She had a knee-jerk reaction, exclaiming, "Love gives you something, compassion does not." I knew she was wrong and that her view was selfish, but I couldn't debate the issue just then. All she wanted was a few minutes' worth of diversion. I needed more time to consider the elements. I knew that love, compassion and devotion are all ultimately the same. I didn't know how to effectively explain that to her in a few short moments.

The puzzle I was solving was, where does love go when the object of one's affection no longer exists? The most important question: Is love on the material plane possible at all or do we just cling and call that love? Leaving Buddhism behind, I knew compassion was not the whole picture. Compassion is a quality that arises from a loving heart. A loving heart comes from one's soul. If the soul is an unknown force within, confusion takes place. Therefore, what we think of as love and compassion are the same and, at the same time, they are different in their quality.

I was beginning to see that love, turned inward with no place to go or no expression, creates depression and self-loathing. EUREKA!!! I was onto something big! A gigantic leap in time and space came next. Love simply exists. It is. It is prana, it is air, it is cellular, and it is our natural state. It is our soul's expression. It is what we all want, but it is not who we ALL are. We can transmigrate downward. We can slowly diminish our capacity for love. We can become demonic. Therefore, love must be cultivated through thought, actions and nourishment.

When love has no expression, we are miserable or miserly. Ouch, that hurts! I was getting it. I knew then why the power of artistic expression heals. I knew that art is the soul's expression. It is a way to release itself, a way for others to have the treasures and gems we store within the chambers of our true heart. It's like releasing a valve that's about to burst. Love can transform into art. It can be understood and cherished by those whose hearts are open and able to parse the message of the artist. The Pink Adobe Guest House was my loving expression.

Krishna loves creativity. What I did, for the pleasure of all, I could not deny; nor could I look at it until I understood these distinctions. I had to get to the source. I had to separate materialism from spiritualism. Tommy's guest house, though it is material, has soulful qualities because it had been created with love. It has a personality. Now, when I walk that way and dare to look, I say to myself, that is a loving expression. It's a tribute to God. It came from my heart. I began to regain confidence and feel good again. My heart no longer closed up or tightened against itself. LOVE DOESN'T GO AWAY. LOVE EXISTS, REGARDLESS OF ONE'S STATE OF MIND. When we do not understand our relationship with God, we suffer. When we do not understand that self-expression is a form of devotion to God, we suffer.

I was ready for a complete understanding and makeover. I had to admit that I still loved Tommy, though we were not suitable for each another. Love, in the service of God, for Krishna's pleasure, is eternal. After all Tommy is a soulful spirit, albeit misguided and not yet ready for prime time!

> *"A person who has developed detachment can give up the bondage of material society, friendship and love. And a person who undergoes great suffering gradually becomes, out of hopelessness, detached and indifferent to the material world. Thus, due to my great suffering, such detachment awoke in my heart; yet how could I have undergone such merciful suffering if I were actually unfortunate? Therefore, I am, in fact, fortunate and have received the mercy of the Lord. He must somehow or other be pleased with me."*
> —*(Srimad Bhagavatam 11.8.38)*

After Tommy and I had split up, Krishna began to bestow considerable mercy on me. Many of the unfinished, unexplainable circumstances of my life were coming to abrupt and dramatic endings. Later on, in reflection, my friend Krsna-Kumari said to me, "Donna, Krishna was picking all the fleas off of you." Thinking about that, I could easily visualize myself, a forlorn dog, sitting on the doorstep. I did not realize that I was being freed from affiliations and attachments that did not serve my service to the Lord. I felt Krishna's hand on my shoulder but I didn't know where he was leading me. I might have been afraid of the emptiness but Buddhist practice had taught me to sit quietly in whatever arises. How was I to know that I was about to embark on a rocket ride out of this stratosphere?

At that time, I went to see an intuitive acupuncturist in Tucson. His treatments were vital in my resurrection. Seeking higher ground, my spirit began to realign with his needles. The turning point came after I had restored my diet to its spiritual foundations (no flesh and very little processed food). After one appointment with Charlie Roach, I remembered that Govinda's Natural Foods Buffet was just around the corner from his office. As I drove toward the Hare Krishna restaurant, I realized that something was changing, and after parking my car and walking toward the pink and turquoise café, I asked myself, why had it taken me so long to come back here? When I first moved to Arizona, I often ate at Govinda's and then for some reason time elapsed and many years had passed.

After visiting Govinda's restaurant a few times, I began to attend the Sunday evening program. I came with Bhagavad-gita in hand. I relished the detailed instructions Krishna gave Arjuna on how to be a first-class devotee. Admittedly, having spent so many years on various Buddhists pathways, from the

Theravada to the Vrajayana, I needed to understand why I was losing interest in Buddhism. Doing my research, I found an article by Steven J. Rosen, an initiated disciple of A.C. Bhaktivedanta Swami Prabhupada. His compassionate essay on Buddhism and Vaishnavas addressed my confusion.

In a nutshell, Vaishnavas, Krishna's devotees, know that God is a personal being who is reciprocal and relational—a being that is all knowledge, all power, supreme in strength, and unequaled in attractiveness. I was relieved in my realization that there is a reason why I am here on this planet at this time and that my unique character and attributes are not a random whim of nature to be erased by time. Buddhist nihilism, on the other hand, makes life on this planet seem like a punishment that we must endure before we might merge into the vast Buddha field, otherwise known as the Brahma Jyoti. While Buddhists endure and abide, Vaishnavas create and serve.

Encouraged, I emailed him and was further inspired by his rapid reply. He recommended that I find his out-of-print book, *From Nothingness to Personhood,* a scholarly understanding of the nature of Buddhism explaining why the Buddha came to this Earth as an Avatar of Krishna the Supreme Being. Krishna was leading me back to Godhead. Satyaraja's (Rosen's initiated name, meaning "King of Truth") outstretched hand and willingness to help me, an unknown e-mailer, affirmed the truth of the International Society for Krishna Consciousness. Every Jiva, every soul, is important. After crawling through barren land, thirsty for true Nectar, I had come to the abundant oasis. I had that incredible Eureka feeling. Hallelujah, Holy Moses, sweet Jesus, and HARE KRISHNA. Bells were ringing. In a very brief time, I unearthed a gold mine of spiritual scholarship and was having myriad realizations, both spontaneous and from hearing and reading Prabhupada's commentaries. I began to sparkle. I found my Holy Grail!

GIRIRAJ SWAMI

One hot summer afternoon, His Holiness Giriraj Swami came to Govinda's to give a Brahmin initiation to his disciple, Ananta Deva Das. Ananta, who was preparing the temple grounds for the arrival of his guru, asked the few of us who were present to participate in welcoming Giriraj Swami to Govinda's. I was on the premises early that Sunday afternoon to attend a meeting. When the door to the meeting room opened and in walked Giriraj Swami, everyone scrambled from his or her seat to pay obeisances. Although disappointed by past spiritual leaders, I followed along, expecting little. Perhaps I was in a spiritual stupor from my experiences with the numerous high-hatted, high-seated, throne-seeking, self-aggrandizing, narcissistic gurus I had encountered. Once we settled back into our seats, Giriraj Swami earnestly asked each of us where we were on our individual spiritual path. Now, my antennae were up. I watched him listen attentively as we told our small stories. I was impressed seeing that Giriraj Swami was sincerely interested.

ISKCON's Sunday program usually begins at 5:30 p.m. with a half hour of Kirtan, followed by a half-hour talk, that is followed by a half-hour celebration of the Lord's holy name, an aarti. Giriraj Swami began his talk by sharing the opening of one of his recent books, *Watering the Seed*. We all laughed while he told us about his efforts to find a true guru. Fortunately for all of us, it was a relatively short journey for him to the lotus feet of Srila Prabhupada. Upon meeting Srila Prabhupada, he quickly left his materialistic life behind. Glenn Teton became Giriraj and then, after years of unalloyed devotional service to the Acharya founder of the International Society for Krishna Consciousness, he became Giriraj Swami.

The Sunday program always concludes with a feast. It was late summer and Sandamini, the temple's founding president, was in India. The vibe was homey and familiar. I was enjoying my associations and dinner on the patio while Guru Maharaj visited with others indoors. When it was time for me to head home, I noticed Giriraj Swami in the temple hall with only one other person. I decided to go in and pay my personal respect to His Holiness. I began to ask him questions about his experiences and he pointed me toward his two most recently published books: *Watering the Seed* and *Life's Final Exam.* I told him that I was going to India soon and intended to stay in Vrindavan for five weeks. He asked me my purpose in Vrindavan and I honestly told him, with a bit of wit and humor, that I intended to observe ISKCON from "the other side of the road." He laughed. I didn't realize how foolish I was, but everything was changing for me so rapidly it was hard to keep up. I was flying by the seat of my pants with more courage than intelligence. My decision to go to Vrindavan was illogical, untimely and unexpected.

If life were scripted, there would be no need for faith. As such, it is not. After all the dramatic conclusions I recently experienced and after staring into what I once considered the path of liberation—namely, impersonalism and voidism—I rapidly embraced Krishna Consciousness. Every spiritual question I had was being answered. Most importantly— the nameless quality missing in my past had a name.

When my realization came that it was time to go across the world into Krishna's cowherd territory, I listened, I considered, and I made sure I was not having a manic moment. When I felt completely sure that I was being divinely guided, I booked the trip. At long last, I had arrived on a spiritual path that made complete sense to me and it was rapidly carrying me aloft. Guru Maharaj asked me more questions: Where was I going to stay? How long would I be gone? What did I intend to do while there?

I told Giriraj Swami that I intended to stay at the Jiva Institute because ISKCON's guest house and hotel were fully booked. I was being guided to Vrindavan at the end of Kartik, a holy month when pilgrims and devotees from all over the world would converge on Krishna's boyhood village. Driving home that evening through the high Sonoran Desert was particularly wondrous. I had a happy heart! I knew Giriraj Swami was the real deal.

I have found the International Society for Krishna Consciousness to be synonymous with intelligence. The once-young, hippy children who became Srila Prabhupada's devoted disciples are now in their senior years; many are learned Sanskrit scholars. A lifetime of devotion and study has made them gurus. Srila Prabhupada encourages everyone to be a guru. Learn, study, recite, teach, and preach. A powerful mainstay of Srila Prabhupada's mission is distributing his books. Steadfastly he translated major texts from the

Vedas, as well as writing purports and commentaries on the *Srimad Bhagavatam,* the *Bhagavad-gita* and other Vaishnava scriptures. Knowing how precious his time on Earth would be, he translated the spiritual knowledge of the Vedas for Westerners in record time. He knew we would carry the message of Krishna Consciousness across the globe and back to Mother India once we understood its importance in these turbulent times.

DIVINE TALES OF THE LORD

"Srimad Bhagavatam is the transcendental science not only
for knowing the ultimate source of everything but
also for knowing our relation with Him and our duty
toward perfection of the human society on the basis
of this perfect knowledge."
—Srila Prabhupada

Every morning in ISKCON temples worldwide there are *Srimad Bhagavatam* classes. These classes are available; anyone can listen through the miracle of Internet networks. The spiritual material is ever fresh, ever rewarding, and ever-changing, to meet us where we are.

Soon after booking my trip I met a devotee who convinced me that I had to purchase the complete set of the *Srimad Bhagavatam. Srimad Bhagavatam* means "Divine-Eternal Tales of The Supreme Lord." To read these books, I found I must follow the regulative principles. I must be immaculate inside and out. I need to study in a designated room where I have privacy. I resisted buying the *Bhagavatam*. I didn't feel ready for it. I did not have an appropriate bookshelf or time to begin it; nor did I feel qualified to own it. The sincere devotee kept up his campaign and I soon surrendered.

A few weeks later the boxed set arrived. Bound with packing tape, it seemed secure enough to stay in its packaging until a bookcase could be built especially for the eighteen volume set. Time went by; the bookcase I ordered never came. I painted the second bedroom in my home and began to make it ready to be the Krishna library. After some time had passed, I began to feel the impetus to open the box, with or without the shelter of a proper case. Now, in a freshly painted, clean, well-lit room, I put my feet up and began.

> *"This Bhagavata Purana is as brilliant as the sun, and it has arisen just after the departure of Lord Krsna to His own abode, accompanied by religion, knowledge, etc. persons who have lost their vision due to the dense darkness of ignorance in the age of Kali shall get light from this Purana." (Srimad Bhagavatam 1.3.43)*

Originally preserved through oral tradition, the Vedas were put into writing by Srila Vyasadeva, the "literary incarnation of God." In the form of *Srimad Bhagavatam*, the compilation is known as "the ripened fruit of the tree of Vedic literature." *Srimad Bhagavatam* is the most complete and authoritative exposition of Vedic knowledge. Disciplic succession begins by initiation under a "spiritual master." The beginning of the *Srimad Bhagavatam*, as well as the *Bhagavad-gita*, emphasizes:

ONE MUST HAVE A SPIRITUAL MASTER to unlock the Vedic doors.

Lord Krishna said: "I am seated in everyone's heart, and from Me come remembrance, knowledge and forgetfulness. By all the Vedas am I to be known; indeed, I am the compiler of Vedanta, and I am the knower of the Vedas."—Bhagavad-gita, 15.15

Once again, there I was, sitting with head in hands, pondering whether a true guru would be possible for me at this stage of my life. Up until that point, every guru, every teacher, every spiritual program had not held up under my scrutiny. Neti-neti. I had many false starts and, now, I was to ask for a bona-fide spiritual master? Would this person truly look out for me? Could I sincerely and faithfully surrender at his Lotus Feet?

I needed to think deeply. Everything thus far in Krishna Consciousness had lined up. For many years I had considered myself a yogi and now I was being shown the next step on the ladder. Pondering the question of surrender to a "spiritual master," I decided to write to Giriraj Swami. His sincerity, his humility, his scholarship, his relationship within ISKCON and his devotional service to Srila Prabhupada were beyond question or doubt. Moving from speculation to action stirred my heart.

I wrote to Giriraj Swami with a preliminary question: Could I ask him to be my perfect spiritual master? I asked him what that would entail and how that might happen. I felt awkward. I was in new territory again.

His humble response, true to his character, could not have been more perfect. He replied that he could not be my perfect spiritual master but he could lead me to him. I felt encouraged. He went on to ask me many questions about my motivations and my upcoming trip to India. I fired off rapid responses as the date of my departure was getting close.

My trip had been booked for some months; complicated arrangements were made for house-sitting, dog sitting and the yoga room. With everything in place, Giriraj Swami's last e-mail to me was the pivotal turning point. He said, if I am to be your spiritual master or preceptor, you must change your plans and spend a minimum of three days in association with me, either at the Dallas temple or the temple in Phoenix or Houston.

Whew. I was stunned. What to do? If I had to pinpoint an exact moment when my actual spiritual life began, it would be that moment. I walked toward the garden, standing on the top step and looked outward. I recognized how crucial my decision would be. All my previous experiences came rushing to the forefront of my mind. I thought about all the money spent following one guru or another. I was reeling from the flood of disappointments rushing so quickly into my consciousness. But I knew I must consent and see what surrendering would entail. I briefly imagined that Giriraj Swami would ask difficult things of me and, for a short moment, I imagined more bitter disappointments. But then, like the airplane Thanat spoke about back in my Vipassana days, I started to lift up. I realized my trip to India routed me through Dallas anyway. All I would have to do is change the day of my departure to three days earlier and the thought of leaving sooner rather than later was the first of many delightful changes and spiritual realizations. Once I turned the corner into acceptance, my life kept getting better and better. I could not imagine the glorious days to come.

ON THE ROAD TO VRINDAVAN

Albert Einstein famously said, "Information is not knowledge. Knowledge is the practical application of information from real human experience." I went to Vrindavan, India, Krishna's transcendental world, to have such an experience.

I arrived in Dallas on October 31, 2014. I was met at the airport by one of Giriraj Swami's young disciples, Vrinda Priya Devi Dasi. With too many suitcases in tow, we headed for the Dallas ISKCON Temple—Radha-Kalachandji—and the generous guest apartment Giriraj Swami had arranged for me. As Guru Maharaj said, I would be well cared for and need not want for anything while there. With extreme thoughtfulness and kindness, Guru Maharaj made different arrangements for my stay in Vrindavan. The Jiva Institute was no longer on my horizon; I now had lodging within ISKCON at the Kirtan ashram for women. I would attend the retreats sponsored by the Vrindavan Institute for Higher Education. Without Giriraj Swami's intervention, I might have been miserable in a noisy, dangerous, crowded little village. But with Giriraj Swami's intervention, and having Sandamini Devi Dasi generously share her Indian phone and all her available contacts, my trip was out of this world.

Before leaving Dallas, Giriraj Swami invited a few of his disciples to the Trammel Crowe Museum where we would see an exhibit of B.G. Sharma's miniature paintings of Krishna and Radha. I bought an iPhone 6Plus just for its wonderful photographic ability. I wanted to bring back, in the way of photographs, as much art as I could. Before climbing the stairs to the Sharma exhibit, we had to walk through an exhibit of retro fashion from the designers I studied when I was a weaver.

Krishna and Radharani had given me gifts beyond my imagining. From the moment I changed my itinerary, my experience grew richer and richer and the Sharma paintings were little miracles that I was allowed to photograph. As I left the museum for the airport, Giriraj Swami told me I was off to an auspicious beginning. Soon after leaving the Trammel Crowe Museum, at Radharani's request, with Krishna's mercy and Giriraj Swami's blessing, I boarded the plane to India.

Eagerly disembarking from a British Airway's flight from North America to India, I arrived in New Delhi exhilarated by the nature of my visit. As I walked down the concourse, I looked up at the giant sculpted-metal hand mudras that are strategically located above eye level to inspire, inform, and welcome us into India's remarkable culture. A few of my acquaintances could not understand why I would cross the globe and trade my comforts and securities for an adventure in such an extreme and often difficult country. I told them to consider me a spiritual archeologist, delving deeply into the culture of Krishna.

Though I traveled alone, I felt encouraged and supported by my new found friends, all devotees within the International Society for Krishna Consciousness. Sandamini Devi made arrangements for me to spend my first two nights in India at the ISKCON guest house. Giriraj Swami continued his merciful kindness by arranging for me to attend two important retreats sponsored by the Vrindavan Institute for Higher Education. After resting for two days in Delhi, I would soon enter the transcendental villages where Krishna spent his youth and childhood, taking care of the cows, loving the Gopis, and uplifting Govardhan Hill with one finger to save the denizens from Indra's wrathful rain.

I was about to begin my third pilgrimage to India. The first one, many years before, I was with Bikram, the second with Dzigar Kongtrul Rinpoche, and now a new experience would unfold.

Though not an expert, I had enough background to know that my Western sensibilities would be shocked when I left the clean, organized airport terminal. Standing at the exit door, I took a deep breath and said to myself, okay now, get ready. I knew once I left the terminal there would be no escaping the noise, chaos and toxic pollution. I had to be on my toes. India is wild. The drivers are wild; the noise level is overwhelming; and the pollution in Delhi is sickening. India, by its very history and nature, is transcendental. What lies above and below the surface are years of spiritual evolution, which continues to intrigue, invite and enthrall—if you can see beyond the grunge.

In the terminal I hired a prepaid taxi to take me to the ISKCON guest house, but the driver had no idea where to find it. He did not speak English and I do not speak Hindi. I kept saying, east of Kailash, Sant Nagar… as though he would understand me if I continued to shout the location from the backseat. Realizing my foolishness, I handed him a paper with the street name and neighborhood carefully printed out. Then, he stopped and consulted another driver and, with only a few false turns we found the street, the entrance and the surrounding gateway.

To be admitted to the guest house vicinity, one's name must appear on a list. After the guards had checked the list and found my name, there was more security to pass through. Frisked by a wand for weapons and other inappropriate paraphernalia, I was cleared to continue. Once on the inside, I faced the daunting task of getting my cumbersome bags up a steep hill and then up three flights of steps to the reception desk. The taxi driver was reluctant to follow along or help with the bags. I had to promise a good tip and give a lot of happy smiling encouragements to get his cooperation.

Successfully navigating all the obstacles, we were finally on the uppermost floor of the guest house where the reception agent was sound asleep. After I gently roused him and introduced myself, he courteously showed us a well-situated room, high above the temple courtyard. Tipping the driver with far more rupees than necessary and a bag of dried mangoes from Trader Joe's, I pushed him out of my room and swiftly locked the door behind me.

It was 3:30 a.m. The morning devotions were to start soon. Arriving at the temple after traveling for twenty-eight hours, to me it seemed a perfect beginning. Mangala-Aarti begins sometime between 4:00 and 4:30 a.m. In this instance,

Mangala refers to the auspicious time of day when one is fresh from a good sleep and the day is still quiet. The altar curtains open and the pujari (temple priest) blows the conch (shankha), awakening the adored deities. The pujari then offers the freshly awakened deities balya-bhoga—water and milk sweets, or other preparations suitable for the early morning. Everyone then takes darshan (holy vision) by gazing at the freshly awakened deities. After a half hour or so, the pujari closes the altar curtain and it is time to worship Tulasi Devi.

"Tulasi is auspicious in all respects. Simply by seeing, simply by touching, simply by remembering, simply by praying to, simply by bowing before, simply by hearing about, or simply by planting this tree, there is always auspiciousness. Anyone who comes in touch with the Tulasi tree in the ways mentioned above lives eternally in the spiritual world."
—Srila Prabhupada, The Nectar of Devotion

In the temple chamber the men and women, in separate circles, worship the holy plant by circumambulating and offering her sanctified water. Then the time comes to begin chanting the HOLY NAME a minimum of 1,728 times. Using a Tulasi wood mala, a necklace of 108 beads that nests securely within a bead bag, one fingers the beads from within the bag privately, dropping a counter bead each time a full round is completed.

HARE KRISHNA, HARE KRISHNA; KRISHNA KRISHNA, HARE HARE; HARE RAMA HARE RAMA, RAMA RAMA HARE HARE!

It is the request of Srila Prabhupada (the Founder-Arcaya of ISKCON) that those who sincerely wish to take initiation in the cult of Krishna chant sixteen rounds of the Maha (great) mantra each day. When one becomes proficient in the devotion, it can be accomplished within two hours. Devotional chanting is the means to purify oneself in this degenerate age of Kali. Chanting Krishna's holy name and performing devotional service minimizes materialist attachments and makes one truly happy!

The ISKCON Temple, East of Kailash, perches on a hill where pathways meander between the guest quarters, resident quarters, restaurant, gift store and a Vedic museum. Surrounding the pink stone carved buildings are gardens, terraces and porticos. The altar room sits at the highest elevation. Climbing the many stairs to the sacred chambers, one comes to a circular portico where a large black stone Garuda stands in its center. Garuda is a giant humanoid bird, part eagle and part man who is the bird-carrier of Lord Vishnu.

In the *Garuda Purana,* Vishnu, the Preserver and Creator of the Universe, informs Garuda of the reason and meaning of life. He gives details of metaphysics and reincarnation. Thus, it is no wonder that Garuda is placed strategically on the portico, as well as on either side of the stairway into the temple chamber.

AT RADHARANI'S REQUEST

After chanting the Hare Krishna mantra sixteen times around the 108-bead mala, I wandered through the temple's grounds. I followed the pathways in front of the Vedic museum, around the gardens and the gift shop, until I found my way back to the entrance of the little guest quarters. I was ready for a rest. My room, well-situated high above the temple's portico, allowed me to blissfully fall asleep, listening to the sweet bhajans that were indistinguishable from my state of mind. As I drifted off to sleep, the ringing temple bells took me further into the transcendental world. Feeling safe, secure, and happy, I slept until a booming voice outside my door announced, "PRASADAM!". I did not know that the guest house would provide sanctified meals three times each day. I turned over and went back to sleep.

In the Chaitanya-charitamrita (Madhya-Lila, 4.93, purport) Srila Prabhupada writes: "The Krishna consciousness movement vigorously approves this practice of preparing food; offering it to the

Deity, and distributing it to the general population. This activity should be extended universally to stop sinful eating habits, as well as other behavior befitting only demons. A demoniac civilization will never bring peace to the world. When the people take to eating only prasadam offered to the Deity, all the demons will be turned into Vaishnavas. It is then and then only that a peaceful condition can prevail in society."

I do not remember how I spent the rest of that day. Perhaps I posted pictures on my Facebook page or wrote in my journal or repacked my bags. Whatever I did, the day went by and hunger eventually drove me out of my room. Still without the realization that meals were available, I found my way down the hill and into the temple's public restaurant. Early for dinner, I observed the wait staff lovingly prepare the tables. I was the first for dinner and the only woman in the restaurant. I was a vulnerable combination of interesting and ignorant. Sitting by the door, I perused the menu. Women are conspicuously absent from the commercial enterprises within the temple walls, but women are the internal force that fuels spiritual life. Radharani is Krishna's most beloved consort, whose shakti, or energy, is the primordial cosmic energy and represents the dynamic forces that move through the entire universe.

While waiting for my meal, the men rearranged the tables, added salt shakers, filled water glasses and tried to appear busy. When not doing small tasks, they huddled together and whispered quietly to one another and stole furtive glances in my direction. I felt a bit self-conscious. Just when I had the uncomfortable feeling that I was being scrutinized, another woman came into the restaurant. Though not traditionally dressed in a sari, she was Indian. Her lustrous long black hair, combined with her Western garb, portrayed poise and courage. As I considered her, she considered me, and after only seconds of studying each other, she confidently asked if she could join me for dinner. Our eyes met in agreement. We were both ready to share stories.

She told me that she was traveling alone and had just arrived by train from Rishikesh. She would be staying overnight while on her way to South India, where she would visit with her elderly father. She was a physician from Montreal. She also told me that she enjoyed traveling through India alone, and I shouldn't worry as long as I was cautious, respectful, and smart! She then asked me the nature of my trip.

I began to recount my recent experience of coming to Krishna Consciousness. I told her about my traumatic relationship with Tommy. I briefly told her how I pondered the nature of love and found my Buddhist spiritual practices insufficient. Continuing, I told her I heard Krishna calling! She was very interested in the events that led up to my pending visit in Vrindavan and the two retreats I might attend.

"Srimai Radharani is a tenderhearted feminine counterpart of the supreme whole, resembling the perfectional stage of the worldly feminine nature. Therefore, the mercy of Radharani is available very readily to the sincere devotees, and once She recommends such a devotee to Lord Krishna, the Lord at once accepts the devotee's admittance into His association.

—(Srimad Bhagavatam 2.3.23)

The kindly woman assured me that I would be perfectly safe within India, because, "Donna, you are here at Radharani's request!" She continued to tell me to always think of Radharani and look for her because she would appear to me in various ways.

The following day I began to feel the jet lag but wouldn't surrender to the fatigue. I took myself, via riksha, to the National Gallery of Modern Art, situated near the India Gate on the government circle. Once inside the multistoried museum filled with India's modern painted treasures, I found my way to the lowest level, where I discovered an extraordinary impressionist painter, Amrita Sher-Gil. Born in Budapest, Hungary, her father was a Sikh aristocrat who was a Sanskrit and Persian scholar, and her mother, Marie Gottesmann, was a Jewish opera singer from Hungary.

I found Sher-Gil's heritage interestingly relatable. In the many years I had painted, my style was impressionistic and, with discovering Sher-Gil, an inquiry into my past became known. She, her parents and her style of painting were familiar to me. Unfortunately for me, no photos were allowed, and the reproductions online do not do the paintings justice. Sher-Gil's life was tragically short. She died before reaching her thirtieth birthday, leaving a large legacy of work that fills the bottom floor of India's National Gallery. I was so thankful that I dragged myself out that afternoon, as meeting Sher-Gil through her paintings seemed to unite me with a missing piece of myself.

RECIPROCATION

No one can explain to you or give you the realization of Krishna or Radharani.

You have to want to believe by having faith, shradda and you have to qualify by following the regulative principals. Chanting the holy name of Krishna has potency and Lord Shri Krishna and Srimati Radharani will reciprocate.

The next day, I arrived in Vrindavan by hired car. After considerable time navigating the narrow passages, we found the Kirtan ashram, which is on one of the main roads in the bustling village. Vrindavan is a mix of ancient temples and modern renovations. In early November it was still quite warm. The closeness of the narrow streets, along with the noise, felt a bit cloying and claustrophobic.

Once we found the entrance to the compound, the driver insisted on making arrangements for my return fare before I could leave the car. Impatiently, we exchanged phone numbers and I agreed to call him for my return trip to Delhi six weeks later. Then we pounded on the metal gate and an older man with a large stick opened the door for us; a young woman with a disarming smile quickly followed him. Jaya Mati was the second-in-command while Visakha devi, a disciple of Giriraj Swami, was away.

The gatekeeper's job also entailed keeping marauding monkeys at bay. The watchman and the driver both carried all my bags to the third-floor room. (I will never travel to India again with more than one medium-sized suitcase.) Each landing was enclosed with an iron gate and heavy-gauge screening. Before coming to Vrindavan, I was forewarned about the dangers of the monkeys and, as I looked around, I realized keeping them at a safe distance was essential for my safety. I was told to hide food while in transit and never look them in the eyes; ignore them with confidence was the mood to have when dealing with monkeys anywhere, in or out of the village.

Once in the room I felt some relief. The dark-brown walls, plastered with cow dung, along with the black plantation shutters and a glossy dark green door, made the room look and feel like one of Amrita Sher-Gil's paintings. My quarters were spacious, with a large bathroom and a small kitchen. The apartment had screened patios, both in front and back.

It had been a long journey from Tommy to Vrindavan. I just wanted time to settle in, take a deep breath, open my books and chant the many rounds on my mala, but the very next day I was to leave by bus for the first of the two retreats. I had not considered where or how I would eat and I spent the remainder of the day packing and repacking my things. Not knowing what I might need and not wanting to take too much, I could only nervously speculate. I was not yet comfortable in a sari, the preferred dress for devotees; my clothing was a mix of brightly colored fabrics from East and West.

That night, the street noise and the screaming monkeys kept me awake. The next morning, I had to figure out where to meet the bus. Once on the sidewalk with my bag trailing behind, I followed two other retreat-goers who were also on their way to meet the bus. The number of devotees attending this retreat was staggering. There were people from all over the world. In total, there were more than three hundred and fifty of us milling around on a crowded, narrow dusty street with no sidewalks trying to find out which bus we were to take. I was beginning to feel gravity working against me.

THE HARI NAM RETREAT

The ashram we arrived at was large by any standard. It accommodated all of us, with room for more. As everyone needed to receive a room assignment and make last-minute payments, patience was necessary to support the organizer's valiant efforts. I, the last guest to be registered, had a very long wait until my room could be assigned. By then, my hunger and fatigue had taken its toll.

When I approached one of the retreat organizers, she told me to wait until the end and then she would find a suitable room for me. Finding a chair, I took my seat and began the long vigil. Watching everyone find their place, discover their roommates and come back with disagreements or needing to make other arrangements slowed the process. After a while, tears began to roll down my checks, less from despair or a bad attitude than from nervous vulnerability and exhaustion. I hadn't eaten or slept well for many days. While I was sitting in the chair, feeling helpless, a man approached asking what he could do for me. I told him my dilemma and he came back with food.

Soon after, I was called to get my room assignment and meet my roommate, Janaki, a devotee from South Africa chosen specifically for me. Janaki was a young beautiful woman who told me she would look after all my needs and that I was not to worry about a thing. She said that she would show me Radharani's loving kindness; of course, I cried a bit more. She did look as I imagined Radharani might appear.

Srila Prabhupada on Radharani:

"She is the only lovable object of Krishna and She is the Queen of Vrndavana. You will find in Vrndavana, if you go to Vrndavana, everyone is worshipping Radharani. Rani means queen. They are always speaking "Jaya Radhe." Radharani. All the devotees in Vrndavana they are worshipers of Radharani."

The first two days of the retreat, we acclimated to our new surroundings with inspirational classes and Kirtan (responsive singing of the holy name, to the beat of mridanga drums and the rhythm of harmoniums). The day began with the usual morning program, with ample time before breakfast to chant all the rounds.

One morning while standing in the breakfast line, waiting to enter the dining hall, a few of us ladies were in line chanting, perhaps haphazardly, on our beads. Devotees usually carry their beads in embroidered bags everywhere they go. A good devotee always takes every opportunity to chant the holy name. A seasoned male devotee in line behind us said, "Why do you matajis chant this way? A round here and a round there— grabbing a moment between distractions. Do all your rounds in the morning before the program begins and give your chanting your full attention, go deeper, bring your heart to the Japa, make it the focal point of your early morning." Receptive to his message, I allocated specific predawn time for my Japa (chanting) and I was rewarded with a much deeper experience.

A few days later we traveled again by bus, through little villages, along winding roads and up a steep hill to Radha Gardens, where we participated in a twelve-hour kirtan. I didn't know how I would hold up but the day sped by and I loved every minute of it. We were not asked to sit stiffly nor were we made to remain in the music hall. We were free to have the experience in the best possible way for each of us. The beat of the drums, the rhythm of the harmonium, the enthusiasm of the kirtaniya all contributed to a steadily building ecstasy. When we needed a change, we were able to walk around the kund. A kund is an enclosed, architecturally precise body of water used for ritual bathing or swimming. There was a lively atmosphere around the kund, with mischievous children who were friendly, funny but not trustworthy. I enjoyed watching their diversionary antics as they tried to get the best of us and steal a wallet or camera or phone. They did not succeed and, at one point, I told them that they were more bothersome than the monkeys.

My preliminary experiences with Krishna Consciousness were proving to be actualizing. No longer theorizing, my spiritual life was taking on dimensions I had always hoped for. At day's end I found myself asking, is it so strange to think that the Supreme Personality of Godhead walked upon this Earth at various times in our history? Or that the Lord came to this planet as Lord Chaitanya in 1486 to inaugurate the spread of Krishna Consciousness to every village and every town across the globe? Have I been so arrogant in my limited impersonal view to think that I have known the spiritual history or geography of the universe? Did I previously believe that everything came from nothing?

In 1517, Shri Rupa Goswami and Shri Sanatana Goswami, his elder brother, came to Vrindavan village to fulfill four orders of Lord Chaitanya Mahaprabhu (great master). They were to uncover the lost places of Shri Krishna's holy pastimes, install Deities, and establish puja; they were also to write Bhakti-shastras and propagate the principals of Bhakti-yoga.

Our next outing took us to Ter Kadamba, a pilgrimage site where Rupa Goswami fulfilled Lord Chaitanya's request. On this special day of the Hari Nam Retreat, we went to Ter Kadamba to chant 64 rounds of the Maha-mantra. That would amount to 6,912 times. I was intimidated by this formidable undertaking, but my roommate, Janaki, said, "Oh, Mataji, don't worry; we will accomplish this by beginning our day at three-thirty. We will complete at least 16 rounds before breakfast." Encouraged by her youthful but experienced confidence, I was determined.

The skilled bus drivers once again wound their way along the narrow village roads until the enormous vehicles, so out of character for the village streets, arrived at the sacred Kadamba grove where Sri Rupa Goswami wrote texts and verses on Krishna and Radha's pastime. (lilas).

As we entered the grove, gnarled limbs of the Kadamba trees reminded us of their revered history. While we seated ourselves on the ground, the organizers and gurus set up their harmoniums and mridangas under a canopy of the venerated trees. The Kadamba tree figures prominently in Vaishnava literature. Lord Krishna and Srimati Radharani are often depicted in Vaishnava paintings standing under the boughs of the trees while Krishna plays his flute. All around him, the cows, peacocks, the gopis (cowherd girls), and, of course, Radha, ecstatically stand nearby, swelling with pleasure from the Lord's pleasures while the leaves of the Kadamba trees reflect the glow of everyone's love for Krishna.

Disassociation from the material world and starting to understand Krishna's transcendental world is not an aspiration when chanting the holy name; it is an actuality. Chanting the holy name suspends time. The name and the Lord are one and the same. In that sacred space, where I was protected and sheltered, with fierce determination, I did chant 64 rounds of the Maha-mantra. Just as the sun had set, my fingers uncurled from my Tulasi-bead mala and I moved my last bead to its final place.

What a tremendous opportunity Giriraj Swami gave me: No one can take from me the experience I had in Krishna and Radha's villages. With the groundwork in place, we took leave of beautiful Ter Kadamba. No longer a novice, I had the Lord's name securely in my heart. On the bus ride back to our ashram, I remembered Sandamini Devi saying to me, "Donna you are about to go on a rocket ride to the Vaikuntha Planets."

The *Rigveda* (1.22.20) states:

> *Om tad visnoh paramam padam sadā paśyanti sūrayah:* "All the suras (devas) look towards the Supreme Abode of Lord Vishnu," referring to Vaikuntha, the Supreme Abode.

GOVARDHAN

AND THE COWS, THE COWS, THE COWS...

Greatly enthused by the first retreat, realizing the opportunities in front of me, I signed on for the second. In five day's time, we would settle in a village at the foot of Govardhan Hill. The name Govardhana has two primary translations. In the literal meaning, Go translates to "cows", and vardhana translates to "nourishment." Another meaning of Go is "the senses" and vardhana can also mean "to increase." Thus, the name is also translated by devotees of Krishna as "that which increases the senses" in their attraction to Krishna. In this connection, it is believed that by residing in Govardhan and worshipping the mountain, Krishna blesses the devotee by increasing his/her devotion (bhakti).

The footfalls of the great teachers and representatives of the Lord sanctify the dusty pathways surrounding Govardhan Hill. Govardhan is also known as Giriraj, which is another reference to the transcendental mountain where Lord Krishna enjoyed many childhood pastimes. The dust of Giriraj blesses us with Krishna's mercy and informs us of the great teachers, the Acharyas, who have tread on these pathways before us.

After the Hari Nam retreat, I knew a number of devotees who were also staying in Vrindavan between the two retreats. Many of us would have breakfast together in the temple restaurant to discuss the morning *Bhagavatam* class. I kept my days simple by spending the afternoons at the ashram with Visakha Devi, a scholarly woman whose enthusiasm for knowledge was infectious.

When it was time to head to Jatipur Town for the Govardhan retreat, another Giriraj Swami disciple, Nama Cintamini, along with her sister, Jayshree, and I hired a private car and proceeded to the ashram. After finding Nama's room, which was on the main grounds, Jayshree and I were driven to our lodging. We were staying in an ashram not from the retreat center. Due to the worldwide attendance, many of us had to stay in the village. I had mixed feelings about staying off-site, as everything was new to me, and I had a lot to consider.

On the short drive from the retreat center to our ashram, I saw enormous piles of pointed rocks along the roadway. I had a dreadful feeling that very soon those small mountains of rock would be spread along the lane. Though I am a practiced yogini, walking has been my nemesis; with a misshapen sacroiliac joint, I have to be watchful of every footfall. I need to walk straight and purposeful. My determination in the Hatha- yoga room has kept me out of the handicapped category for many years and, when I saw those rocks, I took a deep breath and knew I was about to face a challenge.

When the retreat began, we settled in each morning at the foot of Govardhan Hill under a massive tent. All too soon, trucks began to spread the rocks unevenly on the road between the retreat center and my lodging. Walking back and forth became an extreme sport for me. Even the appointed drivers who were supposed to transport us in the early morning and evening chose not to abuse their vehicles on the treacherous terrain.

While I teetered over the rocks, I had to concentrate on my balance. Fearful of falling and breaking a hip, I went to one of the organizers and pleaded my case. I didn't have much hope for a fruitful outcome, as all the rooms in the village were filled, but I spoke up anyway. The very same woman who arranged for me to have such a wonderful roommate as Janaki listened carefully to my woeful story. Her remedy was to go into Govardhan Village and buy me a walking stick.

Sweet Jesus, Holy Moses, and HARE KRISHNA, what a brilliant solution! With the stick in hand, dressed in a colorful blend of East and West, I made my way over the rocks and stones and, when the children saw me, they called out HARE KRISHNA, HARI BOL while some cried out, "Radhe! Radhe!". Even the monkeys were alerted to their newest danger on the path.

During my early morning stroll to the retreat tent, schoolchildren, dressed proudly in their uniforms with their hair combed impeccably and schoolbags secured on their shoulders, scurried past. Once I got to the crossroads, I often saw a herd of miniature donkeys and families of swine foraging for grub. I saw children and men defecating in the open sewers. I stepped over every manner of dung and, yet, during those short morning walks I was exquisitely happy.

My joy was evident to the villagers whom I passed along the way. One morning, in my colorful, eclectic style,

I met another woman dressed even more colorfully in her traditional style. She had her veil raised over her head, exposing deep-set outlined eyes, making her sensual beauty startling. We stopped in the middle of the road just gazing at each, as though we both saw someone from another realm and another time. We took each other in and we never averted our eyes as we contemplated one another with utter amazement. Wordlessly, we gazed into each others eyes and then, after due consideration, she lowered her veil and disappeared.

I kept my new iPhone 6 Plus close at hand. However, there were a few instances, concerning visions I had that I did not photograph. I will leave it up to you to decide—apparitions, imagination or a causelessly merciful transcendental experience?

After I received the walking stick, I looked forward to the early morning hours and the short walk through the village streets. One morning I turned the corner toward the main road and saw three cows tethered to a wall. Now, these pure-white cows were not ordinary cows. They had enormous black lotus-shaped eyes and were blanketed in decorative robes. I stood very still, spellbound by their loving gaze; unmoving, I could not take my camera from my pocket. I simply breathed the vision in deeply, hoping it would make deep imprints on my mind while praying that I would never forget the spiritual nature of Krishna's Surabhi Cows or the happiness I felt seeing them on my way to the morning program.

From early morning until late at night under the sheltering tent, looking out at Giriraj, the mountain, I listened to enthralling narrations (katha) about Lord Krishna. As Sandamini had promised, I was indeed on a "rocket ride to the Vakhuntha Planets."

THE GEOGRAPHY OF TRANSCENDENCE
BEYOND ORDINARY SENSE PERCEPTION

By the term "unmanifested form" (avyakta-murti), Krishna explains that although He is ever present, we cannot see Him with our gross senses. Srila Prabhupada's commentary illuminates this idea by way of a verse from the Padma Purana, averring that because Krishna's form, qualities, and pastimes are all of a spiritual nature, material senses cannot perceive them. But Prabhupada quickly adds that when a soul in the grip of the material energy is awakened to Krishna consciousness, full understanding and perception of Krishna gradually come to the fore."
—Satyaraja/Steven J. Rosen published in Back To Godhead

"In this world, there is nothing so sublime and pure as transcendental knowledge. Such knowledge is the mature fruit of all mysticism. And one who has achieved this enjoys the self within himself in due course of time."
—(Bhagavad-gita 4.38)

"Krishna also says in the Bhagavad-gita that transcendence is a level of spiritual attainment or a state of being that is open to all spiritual aspirants when they are no longer controlled by base desires and are conscious of a higher spiritual reality."
—Srimad Bhagavatam 10.38.25

padāni tasyākhila-loka-pāla-
kirīt a-jus t āmala-pāda-ren oh
dadarśa gos t he ks iti-kautukāni
vilaks itāny abja-yavāṅkuśādyaih
"In the cowherd pasture, Akrūra saw the footprints of those feet whose pure dust the rulers of all the planets in the universe hold on their crowns. Those footprints of the Lord, distinguished by such marks as the lotus, Barleycorn and elephant goad, made the ground wonderfully beautiful."
—Srila Prabhupada, The Krishna Book

Near the end of our stay at the foot of Govardhan, we heard another katha (narration) from The Krishna Book of Akrura's journey to Govardhan and his ecstatic meeting with Krishna. It goes something like this:

When Akrura arrived in Vrindavan with a message for Krishna, from his enemy Kamsa, Akrura realizing the divine nature of Lord Shri Krishna's footfalls, He, Akrura, disembarked from his chariot and rolled in the dust beneath Krishna's feet.

For our last program, the knowledgeable teachers and retreat leaders had devised a beautiful passage: we were to be showered with the dust of Govardhan while our hearts beat to the rhythms of the harmoniums and mridangas. At the onset of this, like Akrura, my heart leaped from my chest, my hair stood on end, my temperature became erratic and I could not help but cry and tremble with gratitude. Without Giriraj Swami's guidance, I might never have known the glories of Govardhan.

Later that night, when I closed my eyes, images similar to photo negatives rapidly appeared before my eyes. One after the other, they kept coming, until for a brief instant I saw into the blue, electric effulgent realm. The space above my nose and in the empty space between the lines where tilak is drawn, a space opened as if a zipper were pulled slowly downward, and then for a brief instant, a face appeared in the blue light. The next morning when I began to write about my experience, I wrote that it was a different kind of sight. I wrote, my eyes did not see this of themselves and, as I made the journal entry, I realized I was describing an otherworldly "third-eye" vision. If I were ever to have a doubt about Krishna Consciousness, this vision will always evoke the hand of God on my shoulder; it was undeniable. Why I received such causeless mercy is not for me to question or speculate on, but later I was told that Krishna gives you what you need and with that experience I will never fall away or turn back.

Later on, I tried to find information on third-eye visions, pondering how I could share this information in a theoretical way. I found nothing valuable. There are exercises for increasing the effectiveness of the pituitary gland, but I knew, no matter what, that the ego couldn't demand entrance into the Kingdom of Heaven.

I received another taste of extraordinary nectar shortly after the Govardhan retreat ended. Once again at the Kirtan ashram, I attended ISKCON's morning program and followed a simple schedule. One afternoon, Nama Cintamini invited me to visit the nearby goshala (cow sanctuary), along with her sister Jayshree. With my walking stick in hand, we made our way down the sandy lane toward the cows. Nama purchased treats for the young calves and Jayshree and I fed the calves that pushed against each other, competing for our favor. After the supply was gone, I walked away from Jayshree toward a large pasture. Halfway between the corrals and the pasture, I stopped abruptly when I saw a bull leading a line of cows toward a distant field.

This bull had a crown of flowers on his head. He was very, very tall, at least eighteen hands high, if not taller. Words cannot describe how handsome he appeared. As with my Govardhan experience, the iPhone camera was nearby in my pocket but I was again stunned into stillness. I stood motionless, gazing on the most extraordinary bull. After taking in his grandeur, I turned to find my companions so that I could share the sight of this amazing creature. I went swiftly around the corner in search of Jayshree and Nama, but when I found them and we returned to the spot, the bull was nowhere to be seen. I had seen the most extraordinary bull, and I believed the caretakers at the goshala adorned him with the crown and painted his hooves and also placed other markings on his body. So, I told everyone I saw about this extraordinary creature and that they must visit the sanctuary and ask to see him.

The office of the Vrindavan Institute for Higher Education is on the goshala property. I was interested in seeing its base of operations. Therefore, the next day, I asked Visakha Devi to take an afternoon walk with me to see the bull and to visit the institute.

Once at the goshala, Prasanta dasi greeted us and we had a brief tour of the offices and the classroom where the Bhakti Shastra program takes place. Once the tour ended, I asked Prasanta dasi, "Where do they tend the very tall bull?" She replied, "I know of no such bull but I will show you the special Gujarat bull that lives here." So, we went out to a corral and she pointed to the bull that had a very large luminous hump. I commented on his good looks but replied that he was not

the bull I came to see. I was puzzled by this turn of events. After all, I had told everyone about him.

Visakha and I made our way to the little temple where the V.I.H.E cares for its Deities and she recommended that I come back the next day and meditate on why I might have seen Lord Siva's bull, Nandi. Instead of doing that, I took my laptop to the media center on the temple grounds and wrote to Giriraj Swami that I had perhaps had seen Lord Shiva's bull, Nandi, at the goshala.

GIRIRAJ SWAMI'S REPLY

**Shri Vidagda Madhava, "Clever Krishna", Act 6, Autumn
Pastimes, Shri Rupa Goswami**

TEXT 1 (a)
krishnah: sakhe dakshinatah pasya pasya.
tungas tamroru-sringah sphurad-aruna-khuro ramya-pingekshana-
srih
kantha-vyalambi-ganto dharani-vilulitoccanda langula-dandah
so 'yam kailasa-pandu-dyutir atula-kakun-mandalo naicikinam
cakre bhati priyo me parimala-tulitotphulla-padmah kakudmi

TRANSLATION
Krishna: Friend, on the right, look! Look! There is My pet
bull

Padmagandha among the Surabhi cows. He is very tall, and he has
great red horns. His hooves and his beautiful and handsome eyes
are also red, a bell hangs from his neck, his long tail moves on the
ground, he is very tall, he possesses an incomparable hump, and he
is the same white color as Mount Kailasa.

My dear Donna,

Please accept my best wishes.

All glories to Srila Prabhupada.

I am glad that you had such a transcendental visit to Vraja and that you had such good association and such divine experiences there. Surely you have received the mercy of Srila Prabhupada, Sri Giri Govardhana, and their devotees there. Here are some excerpts that may encourage you in your devotion and remembrance of Vraja (the land of Krishna).

"Even today affectionate Lord Krishna enjoys the very sweet nectar of transcendental pastimes there, herding the cows with His brother and His many dear friends. A wonderful sweetness becomes manifest in the heart of they who understand the nectar of this place. Of Vraja, which is more dear even than the city of Mathura, I take shelter." (Vvs 6)

"The hooves of Sri Krishna's Surabhi cows are decorated with sapphires, their horns are studded with gold, and their white cheeks have crippled the pride of the snow-capped mountain peaks. I pray these Surabhi cows may protect us."

"In the company of Balarama and His other friends, and His own body splendidly covered with the dust raised by their hooves, the prince of Vraja daily enjoys a great festival of protecting and milking the cows.

With great happiness He eagerly enjoys pastimes with them in the great forests and on the grand hills and riverbanks of Vraja. Let me worship these Surabhi cows. All glories to Lord Krishna's pet bull Padmagandha, whose handsome horns are covered with gold and studded with jewels, whose hooves are splendidly decorated with sapphires, and whose splendid neck is decorated with a swinging garland of reddish flowers."

"Sometimes Lord Krishna feeds the calves earnestly placing small bunches of tender fresh grass in their mouths, and sometimes He very carefully massages their limbs. I yearn to one day see these calves of Lord Krishna jumping and frolicking in Vrindavan." (Vvs 44-47)

You are truly blessed.

In fact, Srila Prabhupada and Lord Sri Krishna's Mercy blesses us all.

Thank you very much. Yours in service to Srila Prabhupada,

Giriraj Swami

Hare Krishna.

And so my tale of how I came *Up The Ladder* to find service at the foot of Giriraj, by the mercy of His Holiness Giriraj Swami, has come to its end, which is really only a beginning. May of 2016 has been unlike any other time in my life thus far. The culmination of this book, *Up the Ladder*, coincided happily with my initiation into A.C. Bhaktivedanta Swami's family. I am now a true disciple of His Holiness Giriraj Swami and ever grateful to have his shelter.

Your servant,

Her Grace Dana-keli Devi Dasi

Hare Krishna

ACKNOWLEDGMENTS

I thank everyone at Govinda's Hare Krishna Temple in Tucson, Arizona. You opened your hearts to me and allowed me to love you back; for that, I am eternally grateful. I also want to thank my Patagonia community and my yoga students for their open-hearted and open-minded acceptance of all people, like myself, who choose a path less traveled.

Hare Krishna